Industrial Leadership

Driving Transformative Change, Inspiring Success

Liviu Ghiuzan

Copyright © 2025 Liviu Ghiuzan

Published 2025 by VersaCharm Books
email: VersaCharmBooks@outlook.com

ISBN: 978-0-9756456-1-1 (Paperback)

All rights reserved. No part of this publication may be reproduced, distributed, or transmitted in any form or by any means, including photocopying, recording, or other electronic or mechanical methods, without the prior written permission of the publisher, except in the case of brief quotations embodied in critical reviews and certain other noncommercial uses permitted by copyright law.

Preface

Leadership in any industry is both an art and a science, requiring a balance of vision, technical knowledge, and the ability to inspire teams toward a shared goal. Over the years, in my extensive interactions with business leaders across industries, I have observed a recurring challenge that inspired this book. Many leaders, despite their experience and drive, often struggle to bridge the gap between technical understanding and effective leadership. This gap frequently leads to inefficiencies, misaligned priorities, and missed opportunities for innovation.

In countless meetings with business partners and industry professionals, I have encountered situations where the lack of technical vision created barriers to progress. It was not just about understanding the technicalities of their respective industries, but also about how this understanding, or the absence of it, influenced their ability to make strategic decisions, inspire confidence, and drive meaningful change. These moments highlighted a critical need for leaders who excel not only at managing people and processes but also at mastering the technical expertise required to navigate today's rapidly evolving industries.

This book, *Industrial Leadership: Driving Transformative Change, Inspiring Success,* is the result of years of reflection on these challenges. It is designed to empower leaders, whether they are heading a manufacturing company, launching an innovative startup, or steering a global corporation, to combine technical insight with transformative leadership practices. My goal is to provide practical guidance for those seeking to refine their leadership style, strengthen team collaboration, and create a lasting impact on their organizations.

Through the chapters ahead, we will explore the essential principles of leadership, from understanding and connecting with teams to embracing change, fostering innovation, and building a legacy that inspires future generations. Drawing on illustrative case studies and actionable strategies, this book offers insights into addressing common challenges, such as breaking down silos, building resilience, and adapting to disruptive trends.

The industrial landscape is shifting faster than ever due to advancements in technology, global connectivity, and changing employee expectations. To stay competitive, leaders must go beyond traditional management approaches and adopt a mindset of continuous learning and adaptability. Leadership is not a fixed destination but a journey that requires curiosity, humility, and the courage to lead by example.

As you read this book, I encourage you to reflect on your own leadership journey. Consider the strengths you bring, the areas where you can grow, and the legacy you want to leave within your organization. My hope is that this book serves as both a guide and a source of inspiration, helping you become a leader who drives change and inspires success at every level.

Leadership is not a solitary pursuit. It is a collaborative effort built on trust, vision, and shared goals. May the insights and strategies in these pages help you strengthen connections, empower your teams, and lead with purpose and confidence.

Liviu Ghiuzan
Author

Contents

Introduction 1
   Why Leaders in Industry Need a Technical Edge 3
      Balancing Technical Knowledge and Leadership Skills 5
Part 1: Understanding and Connecting with Your Team 9
Chapter 1: Know Your Team's Work, Know Your Team 10
   1.1. The Importance of Understanding Tasks, Tools, and Processes 10
      1.1.1. Identify Strengths and Weaknesses 11
      1.1.2. Recognizing and Addressing the Leader's Weaknesses 17
      1.1.3. Provide Relevant Support 20
      1.1.4. Enhance Decision-Making: Aligning Leadership with Operational Realities 24
   1.2. Gaining Insights Without Micromanaging 29
   1.3. Case Study 1: Understanding Your Team's Work for Better Leadership 32
   1.4. Case Study 2: Empowering Teams Through Awareness and Collaboration 36

Chapter 2: Unlocking Team Potential 42
   2.1. Assessing Strengths, Skills, and Growth Areas 44
   2.2. Aligning Individual Capabilities with Organizational Goals 49
   2.3. Case Study 1: Assessing Strengths, Skills, and Growth Areas in an Industrial Team 54
   2.4. Case Study 2: Aligning Individual Capabilities with Organizational Goals 59

Chapter 3: Humanizing Leadership: Building Bridges Beyond the Workplace 66

- 3.1. Why Team Building Matters 68
- 3.2. Types of Team Building Activities 69
- 3.3. Fun and Meaningful Examples 73
- 3.4. Building Personal Connections 77
- 3.5. Balancing Fun and Productivity 80
- 3.6. Unexpected Benefits 83
- 3.7. Leadership in Action: Stories of Impact 86

Part 2: Driving Change and Growth 91

Chapter 4: Challenging the Status Quo 92

- 4.1. Rethinking "How It's Always Been Done": The Leader's Role in Questioning Norms 93
- 4.2. Creating an Innovation-Driven Environment 97
- 4.3. Strategic Risk-Taking: Balancing Tradition and Progress 102
- 4.4. Leadership in Disruption: Adapting to Change as a Competitive Advantage 107
- 4.5. Case Study 1: Transforming Legacy Processes in Manufacturing – A Leader's Role in Questioning Norms ... 112
- 4.6. Case Study 2: Reinventing a Retail Giant – The Journey of AlphaMartX 116

Chapter 5: Navigating Challenges and Building Resilience 122

- 5.1. Managing Interpersonal Conflicts 124
- 5.2. Bridging Skill Gaps for a High-Performing Team 128
- 5.3. Overcoming Resistance to Change 131
- 5.4. Cultivating a Growth Mindset in the Team 135

5.5. Resilience as a Team Superpower 140

5.6. Case Study 1: Transforming a Team through Skill Development and Conflict Resolution 144

5.7. Case Study 2: Building Team Resilience to Navigate an Industry Shift 147

Part 3: Leading by Example 153

Chapter 6: Leading with Authenticity and Purpose 154

6.1. Walking the Talk: Actions Speak Louder Than Words 155

6.1.1. Authenticity as the Foundation of Leadership 156

6.1.2. The Impact of Consistent Actions 159

6.1.3. Modeling Desired Behaviors in Practice 162

6.2. Humility as a Leadership Superpower 164

6.3. Transparency and Open Communication 168

6.4. Fostering Purpose and Meaning 172

6.5. The Ripple Effect of Authentic Leadership 175

6.6. Case Study 1: From Challenges to Triumph: How Authentic Leadership Transformed Best ClothingXYZ 178

6.7. Case Study 2: From Stagnation to Innovation: The Leadership Journey of Elisabeth Emberhall 183

Chapter 7: From Good to Great Leadership 188

7.1. The Evolution of Leadership: From Competence to Excellence 189

7.2. Building a Culture of Continuous Improvement 192

7.3. Self-Reflection and Feedback: The Pillars of Personal Development 196

7.4. Metrics of Leadership Success: Measuring What Matters
.... 199

7.5. The Legacy of Leadership: Inspiring Future Generations 202

7.6. Case Study 1: Mike's Leadership Revolution at Foods XYZ Co 206

7.7. Case Study 2: Transforming Health Devices XYZ – From Industry Player to Innovator 210

Conclusion: A Call to Action 215

About The Author 219

Introduction

In today's fast-changing market, companies face constant pressure to stay competitive and innovate. To succeed, businesses need leaders who can navigate this challenging landscape while fostering growth and progress. This has created a growing demand for leaders with a unique combination of skills: strong leadership abilities paired with a solid technical background. These leaders can effectively bridge the gap between strategic objectives and the technical realities of their industries, ensuring that innovation aligns with company goals.

But finding such leaders is not easy. Leadership and technical expertise together form a rare combination, and not every candidate fits this mold. In many cases, companies struggle to find leaders who truly understand the complexities of the industry and the work their teams do. When this happens, businesses sometimes hire leaders from other successful companies, even if those leaders lack specific industry experience. While these individuals may excel in general leadership, their unfamiliarity with the technical aspects of the business can become a challenge. Without this knowledge, they might miss critical details, misunderstand team needs, or make decisions that are not well-suited to the industry.

The risks of this misalignment can be significant. Leaders who lack the right technical foundation may find it harder to earn the trust and respect of their teams. Teams often feel more confident and motivated when their leader understands the tools, processes, and challenges they face daily. Without this connection, even strong leaders might struggle to inspire or drive optimal performance.

Furthermore, a lack of technical knowledge can lead to decisions that overlook important details or fail to account for industry-specific complexities. This can slow progress, create inefficiencies, or even put the organization at risk of falling behind competitors who have more aligned leadership. In the fast-paced world of modern industry, there is little room for such missteps.

On the other hand, leaders with a technical edge are better equipped to make informed decisions that align with both strategic goals and the realities of their teams. They can identify opportunities for improvement, spot potential risks early, and collaborate more effectively with technical staff. This not only enhances team performance but also strengthens the organization's ability to adapt to change and stay ahead in the market.

This book explores why having leaders with technical expertise is essential in industrial settings. It also examines how the right balance between technical knowledge and leadership skills can unlock the full potential of a team and an organization. By understanding this balance, companies can ensure they are not just surviving but thriving in a fast-changing world.

In the chapters ahead, we will discuss what it takes to be a successful industrial leader, how to connect with your team, drive change, and lead by example. This journey begins with a deeper look at why technical understanding is such a crucial element of leadership in today's industrial landscape.

Why Leaders in Industry Need a Technical Edge

Industrial leaders are tasked with steering their organizations through environments that are often complex, fast-paced, and highly technical. In these settings, having a technical edge is not just an advantage, it is a necessity. Here's why:

1. Bridging the Gap Between Strategy and Execution

A leader with technical expertise can effectively translate strategic objectives into actionable plans. They understand the specific tools, processes, and constraints their teams face, enabling them to make decisions that are realistic and achievable. Without this understanding, there is often a disconnect between high-level strategies and the day-to-day realities of execution, leading to inefficiencies and missed opportunities.

2. Building Credibility and Trust

Team members are more likely to respect and trust a leader who understands their work. When leaders are knowledgeable about the technical aspects of their industry, they can engage in meaningful discussions, provide relevant guidance, and offer support that resonates with their teams. This credibility fosters stronger relationships and motivates employees to perform at their best.

3. Identifying Opportunities for Innovation

Industries are constantly evolving, and innovation is key to staying competitive. Leaders with a technical edge are better equipped to spot emerging trends, understand new technologies, and evaluate their potential impact. They can guide their teams in adopting innovative solutions and staying ahead of competitors.

4. Making Informed Decisions

Technical knowledge allows leaders to evaluate data, assess risks, and weigh options with a deeper understanding of their implications. This leads to more informed decision-making, particularly in situations where technical challenges or opportunities play a significant role.

5. Navigating Challenges Effectively

Every industry comes with its own set of challenges, whether they involve technical issues, process inefficiencies, or external pressures. Leaders with technical expertise are better equipped to diagnose problems and develop effective solutions. They can also anticipate potential obstacles and plan proactively to address them.

6. Driving Team Performance

When leaders understand the technical aspects of their teams' work, they can provide more targeted support and remove barriers to success. This not only enhances productivity but also boosts morale, as team members feel valued and understood.

In summary, a technical edge empowers leaders to align their teams' efforts with organizational goals, foster innovation, and overcome challenges with confidence.

While leadership skills are vital, they are most effective when paired with a deep understanding of the technical environment in which an organization operates. In the next section, we will explore how to balance technical expertise with leadership skills to achieve optimal results.

Balancing Technical Knowledge and Leadership Skills

While technical expertise is a vital component of industrial leadership, it is only one part of the equation. Leadership is fundamentally about guiding and inspiring others, and technical skills alone cannot accomplish this. Striking the right balance between technical knowledge and leadership abilities is essential for leaders who aim to achieve lasting success.

1. Understanding the Role of Leadership

Leadership is about more than directing tasks or solving problems. It involves setting a vision, fostering collaboration, and creating an environment where team members can excel. A leader's primary responsibility is to empower their team to succeed, and this requires strong interpersonal skills, emotional intelligence, and the ability to inspire trust and confidence.

2. Knowing When to Lead and When to Delegate

A technically skilled leader may feel tempted to dive into the details of every project or solve problems personally. While this can be beneficial in certain situations, it is important to know when to step back and delegate responsibilities. Trusting your team to handle technical challenges allows you to focus on higher-level strategic goals and ensures that team members have opportunities to grow and develop their own expertise.

3. Communicating Effectively Across Levels

Balancing technical and leadership skills requires the ability to communicate effectively with a diverse range of stakeholders. This includes translating technical information for non-technical audiences and ensuring that team members understand how their work contributes to broader organizational objectives. Clear, empathetic communication is key to building alignment and fostering collaboration.

4. Developing Leadership Skills Alongside Technical Expertise

Strong leaders recognize that learning is a lifelong process. Just as technical knowledge must be kept up-to-date, leadership skills also require continuous development. This might involve seeking feedback, attending leadership training, or studying successful leaders within and outside of your industry. By investing in personal growth, leaders can ensure they are equipped to meet the demands of their roles.

5. Balancing Confidence and Humility

Technical expertise can provide a leader with confidence, but it is equally important to remain humble and open to learning from others. No leader knows everything, and the ability to listen, seek input, and admit when you don't have all the answers is a critical component of effective leadership. This humility fosters a culture of collaboration and mutual respect within the team.

6. Focusing on the Big Picture

While technical knowledge helps leaders understand the details, leadership requires a focus on the bigger picture. This means aligning team efforts with organizational goals, anticipating future challenges, and ensuring that the team is prepared to adapt to changes. By balancing technical insights with strategic thinking, leaders can guide their organizations toward sustainable success.

In conclusion, balancing technical knowledge and leadership skills enables industrial leaders to excel in their roles. By integrating these two aspects, leaders can make informed decisions, inspire their teams, and drive innovation while staying focused on long-term goals. In the next chapter, we will explore how understanding and connecting with your team forms the foundation of effective leadership.

Part 1: Understanding and Connecting with Your Team

"A leader who knows their team's work knows their team's worth."

Chapter 1: Know Your Team's Work, Know Your Team

1.1. The Importance of Understanding Tasks, Tools, and Processes

Leadership in any field requires more than vision and strategy; it demands a profound connection to the work being done by the team. At its core, effective leadership begins with understanding the tasks, tools, and processes that drive success. This understanding is not about mastering every detail or micromanaging every step but about cultivating a level of knowledge that bridges the gap between strategic goals and operational realities.

In industries where specialized skills, technical expertise, and precision are critical, this connection becomes even more vital. Leaders who understand the complexities of their team's work can:

- Build trust and credibility by demonstrating respect for the contributions of their team.
- Make decisions that are realistic, informed, and aligned with the team's capabilities.
- Act as true partners in problem-solving, resource allocation, and innovation.

On the other hand, leaders disconnected from the work face challenges such as miscommunication, misaligned priorities, and missed opportunities for improvement. Without insight into the day-to-day realities of their teams, they risk setting unrealistic expectations, failing to provide adequate support, or unintentionally undermining morale.

This subchapter explores why understanding tasks, tools, and processes is a cornerstone of great leadership. It examines how this understanding enables leaders to identify strengths and weaknesses, recognizing and addressing the leader's weaknesses, provide relevant support, and enhance decision-making. Each of these elements is key to creating a high-performing team that is not only effective but also motivated and engaged.

1.1.1. Identify Strengths and Weaknesses

Understanding the Importance of Identifying Strengths and Weaknesses

Every individual on a team brings unique skills, experiences, and perspectives to the table. Identifying these strengths and weaknesses is a critical responsibility for leaders because it allows them to allocate tasks effectively, foster professional growth, and address gaps that could hinder the team's success.

Strengths are the capabilities that allow team members to excel in their roles. These may include technical skills, problem-solving abilities, communication skills, or creativity. Weaknesses, on the other hand, represent areas where a lack of knowledge, experience, or confidence might limit a person's contributions. Identifying and addressing these areas is not about criticism but about creating opportunities for improvement and support.

How Understanding Strengths Enhances Team Performance

When leaders recognize and leverage the strengths of their team members, they can:

- Increase Efficiency: Assigning tasks based on individual strengths ensures that work is completed faster and with higher quality.
- Boost Morale: Acknowledging and utilizing strengths validates team members' abilities, increasing their confidence and motivation.
- Encourage Innovation: Team members working in their areas of expertise are more likely to think creatively and contribute innovative solutions.

For example, a team member who is highly detail-oriented may excel at quality control or auditing tasks, while someone with strong interpersonal skills might be ideal for client-facing roles. By matching the right people to the right tasks, leaders can maximize productivity and job satisfaction.

Addressing Weaknesses for Growth

While strengths drive success, weaknesses often represent untapped potential. Leaders who identify and address weaknesses constructively can:

- Foster Development: Providing training or mentorship opportunities can help team members overcome their limitations.

- Improve Collaboration: Understanding individual weaknesses allows leaders to build complementary teams where members support one another.
- Reduce Risk: Addressing skill gaps or knowledge deficiencies prevents costly errors or delays.

For instance, if a team member struggles with time management, a leader might introduce tools or strategies to help them stay organized. Similarly, if someone lacks technical expertise, targeted training sessions can provide the necessary skills.

Methods for Identifying Strengths and Weaknesses

Leaders can use several methods to assess their team's capabilities:

1. One-on-One Conversations:
   - Schedule regular check-ins with team members to discuss their work, goals, and challenges.
   - Ask open-ended questions to understand their perspectives, such as:
     - "What tasks do you feel most confident performing?"
     - "What areas do you think you need more support or training in?"
2. Performance Reviews:
   - Use structured evaluations to assess individual contributions and areas for improvement.
   - Collect feedback from peers to gain a more holistic view of each person's strengths and weaknesses.

3. Observation:
    - Spend time observing how team members perform their tasks in real-world settings.
    - Look for patterns in behavior, such as problem-solving approaches or communication styles.
4. Self-Assessments:
    - Encourage team members to reflect on their skills and areas for growth through self-assessment tools or questionnaires.
    - Provide prompts like:
        - "What aspects of your work do you find most challenging?"
        - "What skills would you like to develop further?"
5. Team Feedback:
    - Facilitate team discussions where members can share their observations and insights about each other's strengths and contributions.
    - Promote a culture of constructive feedback that focuses on growth rather than criticism.

Leveraging Strengths and Addressing Weaknesses in Practice

Once a leader has a clear understanding of their team's strengths and weaknesses, they can take actionable steps to support them:

1. Tailored Task Assignments:
   - Assign responsibilities that align with each person's strengths, while providing opportunities to address their weaknesses.
   - For example, a strong writer could draft reports, while someone developing technical skills might shadow a senior team member on a project.
2. Mentorship and Training:
   - Pair less experienced team members with mentors who can guide them in specific areas.
   - Invest in professional development programs, workshops, or online courses to build skills across the team.
3. Building Complementary Teams:
   - Create diverse teams where individual strengths offset others' weaknesses.
   - For instance, a team combining analytical thinkers and creative problem-solvers can approach challenges from multiple angles.
4. Setting Realistic Goals:
   - Use knowledge of strengths and weaknesses to set achievable goals that stretch team members without overwhelming them.

Challenges and How to Overcome Them

Identifying strengths and weaknesses isn't always straightforward. Leaders may encounter obstacles such as:

- Resistance to Feedback: Some team members may be hesitant to share their weaknesses for fear of judgment.
- Blind Spots: Leaders may overlook certain capabilities or areas for improvement due to bias or lack of awareness.
- Dynamic Changes: Team strengths and weaknesses can evolve over time, requiring continuous reassessment.

To overcome these challenges, leaders should:

- Foster a culture of openness and trust where team members feel safe discussing their abilities.
- Use objective tools and data to support assessments, such as project outcomes or skill tests.
- Revisit evaluations periodically to adapt to changes in roles, projects, or individual growth.

Conclusion

Identifying strengths and weaknesses is a foundational step in effective leadership. It enables leaders to make informed decisions, allocate resources wisely, and create a supportive environment where everyone can thrive. By investing time and effort in understanding their team's capabilities, leaders not only enhance performance but also build stronger relationships and a more cohesive, motivated team.

1.1.2. Recognizing and Addressing the Leader's Weaknesses

The Value of Self-Awareness in Leadership

Great leaders understand that they are not immune to weaknesses. Just as they identify and address the strengths and weaknesses of their teams, they must also turn the lens inward. Recognizing one's limitations and taking proactive steps to improve is not a sign of weakness—it is a hallmark of strength and resilience.

When leaders assess their own capabilities, they can:

- Bridge Gaps in Expertise: By identifying areas where they lack technical or industry-specific knowledge, leaders can seek training, mentorship, or hands-on experience to enhance their effectiveness.
- Strengthen Team Dynamics: Acknowledging weaknesses fosters trust and transparency, encouraging the team to contribute their strengths to complement the leader's limitations.
- Lead by Example: When leaders commit to self-improvement, they inspire their teams to adopt a similar growth mindset.

Aligning Self-Development with Industry Needs

Industries are constantly evolving, and leaders must stay ahead of these changes. This requires a commitment to continuous learning and a willingness to step out of the office and into the field. Leaders who immerse themselves in the technical aspects of their industry gain valuable insights that:

- Enhance Credibility: Teams respect leaders who take the time to understand the complexities of their work.
- Inform Strategic Decisions: Firsthand knowledge of technical details enables leaders to make more informed and realistic decisions.
- Foster Innovation: Engaging with the production floor, tools, and processes sparks ideas for improvement that may not be apparent from a distance.

Strategies for Leaders to Identify and Address Their Weaknesses

1. Seek Feedback:
    - Encourage honest feedback from team members, peers, and mentors about areas where improvement is needed.
    - Ask questions such as:
        - "Are there aspects of the work that you think I should learn more about?"
        - "How can I better support you in achieving your goals?"
2. Conduct a Self-Assessment:
    - Reflect on your skills and knowledge in relation to the team's strengths and the industry's demands.
    - Use tools like SWOT analysis (Strengths, Weaknesses, Opportunities, Threats) to map areas for growth.

3. Invest in Learning:
   - Attend workshops, industry conferences, or technical training sessions to build expertise in key areas.
   - Shadow team members or spend time in the field to gain a deeper understanding of day-to-day operations.
4. Leverage Team Strengths:
   - Delegate tasks that align with team members' strengths while learning from their expertise.
   - Collaborate with technical experts to gain insights into complex challenges or innovative solutions.
5. Set Personal Development Goals:
   - Create a clear roadmap for improvement with specific, measurable objectives.
   - Examples might include mastering a new software tool, gaining certification in a relevant field, or dedicating time each week to learning about industry trends.

Balancing Leadership and Learning

While it is important for leaders to address their weaknesses, this process should not detract from their primary responsibility to guide and support the team. Striking a balance between self-improvement and leadership duties ensures that the leader remains effective and accessible while pursuing growth.

1.1.3. Provide Relevant Support

The Role of Support in Industrial Leadership

In industrial settings, where operations often involve intricate machinery, tight schedules, and rigorous safety standards, the role of leadership is pivotal. Effective support from leaders is not just an added advantage—it's a necessity for achieving organizational goals. Teams thrive when leaders understand their challenges and provide thoughtful solutions. This requires more than offering generic advice; it demands tailored support that directly addresses the specific hurdles encountered on the production floor or in technical processes.

A supportive leader creates an environment where efficiency, morale, and performance flourish. By addressing issues proactively and equipping their teams with the necessary resources, leaders not only empower their teams but also ensure smoother operations. Supportive leadership builds a foundation of trust and collaboration, enabling teams to perform at their best even in demanding conditions.

Recognizing and Overcoming Challenges

Industrial environments are inherently complex, with each layer presenting its unique set of challenges. Technical demands, such as operating sophisticated equipment or maintaining production quality, often intersect with logistical and interpersonal issues. For example, a delay in parts delivery can cascade into missed deadlines, increased costs, and frustrated teams. Similarly, a lack of access to proper tools or training can hinder productivity and lead to burnout.

Leaders who understand these dynamics are better equipped to remove obstacles. Whether it's streamlining a cumbersome workflow or advocating for additional resources, their actions demonstrate a commitment to supporting their team. This proactive approach not only addresses immediate concerns but also fosters a culture of resilience and problem-solving.

Removing Barriers to Success

One of the most impactful ways a leader can support their team is by identifying and removing barriers that impede progress. These barriers might take the form of outdated equipment, unclear processes, or bureaucratic inefficiencies. For instance, a team struggling with repetitive downtime due to aging machinery needs a leader who will prioritize investment in upgrades or advocate for a more effective maintenance schedule.

In addition, supportive leaders take the time to listen to their teams. Through open communication, they can uncover hidden pain points that may not be immediately apparent, such as conflicting priorities or an excessive workload. Addressing these issues requires a thoughtful balance of empathy, problem-solving skills, and a clear understanding of operational realities.

Providing Tailored Solutions

Offering solutions that genuinely address team challenges is a hallmark of strong leadership. This requires a deep understanding of both the technical and human aspects of the work. For example, when introducing a new system or process, it is not enough to provide theoretical guidance. Leaders must consider the practical implications, ensuring that their teams are equipped with the training and tools necessary for seamless implementation.

Furthermore, collaboration plays a significant role in solution-building. Leaders should create opportunities for team members to contribute their insights, as those working directly with the processes often have valuable ideas for improvement. A leader who fosters this collaborative spirit not only encourages innovation but also strengthens team cohesion and engagement.

The Power of Meaningful Guidance

Beyond solving problems, leaders must provide meaningful guidance that helps their teams grow and thrive. This goes beyond merely giving instructions or setting expectations. Effective guidance involves mentoring, coaching, and offering constructive feedback that builds confidence and capability.

A supportive leader actively seeks opportunities to elevate their team's performance, whether by recognizing individual strengths or by identifying areas for development. For example, if a team member excels at troubleshooting technical issues, the leader might provide additional training to enhance that skill and encourage the sharing of expertise with peers. This creates a ripple effect of improvement, where the entire team benefits from shared knowledge and mutual support.

Guidance also involves clear communication of goals and priorities. When teams understand how their efforts contribute to the bigger picture, they are more motivated and focused. Leaders who articulate a compelling vision and align it with daily operations foster a sense of purpose and drive that extends beyond immediate tasks.

Creating a Culture of Support

Supportive leadership is not just about solving immediate problems—it is about establishing a long-term culture of mutual trust and collaboration. This culture thrives when leaders remain approachable and accessible, taking the time to engage with their teams and understand their needs. Spending time on the production floor, observing workflows, and participating in discussions can uncover insights that might otherwise be overlooked.

By celebrating achievements and reinforcing positive behaviors, leaders further enhance morale and motivation. Acknowledging individual and team contributions demonstrates appreciation and inspires continued effort. Moreover, leaders who continuously seek feedback and adapt their approach ensure that their support remains relevant and impactful as the industry evolves.

Conclusion

Providing relevant support is an essential component of industrial leadership. It involves more than addressing challenges; it requires a genuine commitment to understanding the needs of the team and creating an environment where they can excel. Leaders who prioritize support build teams that are not only productive but also resilient and innovative. This proactive and empathetic approach is the cornerstone of sustained success in industrial settings.

1.1.4. Enhance Decision-Making: Aligning Leadership with Operational Realities

Effective decision-making lies at the heart of impactful leadership, particularly in industrial settings where operational efficiency and strategic alignment are critical. Leaders equipped with a thorough understanding of day-to-day operations are better positioned to make informed decisions that resonate with their team's realities and contribute to organizational success.

Bridging the Gap Between Strategy and Execution

In many industries, a disconnect often exists between high-level strategies devised by leadership and the practical realities of execution on the ground. Leaders who take the time to understand their team's daily tasks, challenges, and workflows bridge this gap effectively. They ensure that decisions are not just theoretically sound but also practically feasible.

For instance, consider a leader in a manufacturing plant facing a decision about introducing new equipment. A leader disconnected from operations might focus solely on cost-saving metrics or technological appeal. However, a leader with a deep understanding of the plant's daily operations would also consider factors like compatibility with existing workflows, employee training requirements, and potential downtime during implementation. This broader perspective results in choices that are both effective and well-received by the team.

Data-Driven Decisions Rooted in Reality

Informed decision-making is increasingly dependent on data, but data alone is not enough. Leaders must contextualize the information by understanding its real-world implications.

Practical Applications:

1. Evaluate Performance Metrics in Context: Operational data, such as production rates or maintenance logs, offers valuable insights. Leaders who understand the context behind these numbers—such as machinery conditions or team workloads—can identify trends and take proactive measures.
2. Prioritize Based on Team Input: When leaders are aware of their team's workflows, they can involve employees in decision-making processes. This collaborative approach not only garners better solutions but also boosts morale by valuing the team's input.
3. Address Challenges Holistically: A leader who knows the intricacies of operations can identify root causes of inefficiencies, ensuring decisions address problems at their source rather than applying superficial fixes.

Balancing Short-Term Needs and Long-Term Goals

A leader grounded in operational realities can better balance immediate needs with strategic objectives. In industrial environments, this often involves making trade-offs between optimizing current processes and investing in future innovations.

For example, during a period of high demand, a production leader might need to decide whether to push existing equipment to its limits or schedule maintenance that could temporarily reduce capacity. An informed leader considers both the immediate impact on output and the long-term risks of equipment failure, arriving at a decision that minimizes disruptions while safeguarding future operations.

Building Confidence and Trust Through Decisions

Leaders who make informed, well-considered decisions earn the trust of their teams. Employees recognize and appreciate when their leader is attuned to the realities of their work, as it demonstrates respect for their expertise and experiences.

Strategies to Enhance Trust:

- Transparency in Decision-Making: Share the reasoning behind choices, including how team input and operational realities influenced the outcome.
- Adaptability: Be willing to adjust decisions as new information arises, showing flexibility and responsiveness.

> Follow-Through: Act on promises and ensure decisions are implemented effectively, demonstrating commitment to both the team and organizational goals.

Practical Steps for Enhancing Decision-Making

To align decisions with operational realities, leaders can adopt several practices:

1. Regular Field Engagement: Spend time on the ground, observing workflows and interacting with team members to gain firsthand insights.
2. Collaborative Problem-Solving: Involve teams in brainstorming sessions to address challenges, combining their expertise with strategic oversight.
3. Scenario Planning: Analyze potential outcomes of key decisions to understand their operational impact before implementation.
4. Training and Development: Continuously enhance personal understanding of operational processes through training and collaboration with technical experts.

Real-Time Decision-Making in High-Stakes Scenarios

Industrial environments often require leaders to make rapid decisions under pressure. A strong grasp of operational dynamics enables leaders to act swiftly without sacrificing accuracy.

For instance, in an emergency such as an equipment failure, a leader familiar with operational workflows can prioritize actions effectively—whether it's reallocating resources, initiating repairs, or communicating with stakeholders. This agility not only mitigates immediate risks but also reinforces the leader's credibility and authority.

Conclusion

In industrial leadership, informed decision-making is a powerful tool for driving success. By understanding the realities of daily operations, leaders can craft strategies that align with both team capabilities and organizational objectives. This alignment enhances team performance, fosters trust, and ensures that decisions resonate from the shop floor to the boardroom.

1.2. Gaining Insights Without Micromanaging

While it is essential to understand your team's work, there is a delicate balance to strike. Too much involvement can lead to micromanagement, which can stifle creativity, reduce morale, and make team members feel undervalued. However, stepping back too far may result in a lack of understanding, misaligned goals, or missed opportunities for support. Striking this balance is key to effective leadership.

Here are some strategies to gain insights without crossing into micromanagement:

1. Ask Questions, Don't Dictate:
   Show genuine curiosity about your team's work by asking thoughtful, open-ended questions. Instead of imposing your perspective, invite team members to explain their processes, challenges, and decision-making. For example:
   - *"What inspired this approach?"*
   - *"How do you think this aligns with our goals?"*
   - *"What roadblocks are you facing, and how can I help?"*

   This fosters a culture of open communication and encourages team members to share valuable insights while preserving their autonomy.
2. Observe Without Intervening:
   Spend time observing how your team operates in their natural workflow. This can include sitting in on meetings, reviewing project updates, or visiting the workspace where tasks are carried out. Focus

on understanding processes and interactions without stepping in to correct or alter their methods. Respect the expertise and initiative of your team members.
3. Hold Regular Check-Ins:
Schedule consistent but brief check-ins to stay informed about progress, challenges, and upcoming tasks. These meetings should be collaborative and focus on understanding team dynamics and needs rather than micromanaging specifics. Use this time to align on objectives and provide high-level guidance.
4. Encourage Team Ownership:
Empower your team to take ownership of their responsibilities. Set clear expectations and trust your team members to deliver. By giving them the space to make decisions, you demonstrate confidence in their abilities, which can increase their motivation and commitment.
5. Leverage Technology for Transparency:
Use collaborative tools to maintain visibility into ongoing projects without excessive oversight. Platforms like project management software allow you to track progress, monitor timelines, and identify potential bottlenecks without disrupting workflows or overburdening team members.

The Leader's Role as a Support System

Understanding your team's work is not just about knowledge—it's about using that understanding to support and elevate your team. Effective leaders act as facilitators who remove barriers, provide resources, and guide their teams toward success. Here's how you can embody this role:

> ➢ Advocate for Resources:
> Once you grasp the tools and processes your team relies on, you'll be better positioned to advocate for resources that enhance their efficiency. Whether it's new software, additional staff, or training programs, understanding your team's needs ensures that you can provide meaningful support.
> ➢ Tailor Your Communication:
> Knowing the nuances of your team's work allows you to communicate more effectively. You can provide feedback that resonates with their experiences, recognize achievements with specificity, and frame challenges in ways that feel relevant and actionable.
> ➢ Lead Problem-Solving Efforts:
> Your insight into your team's processes equips you to address roadblocks collaboratively. By involving your team in solutions and leveraging your knowledge, you can foster innovation and build stronger relationships.

Building Credibility Through Connection

When leaders invest the time to understand their team's work, they not only improve decision-making but also strengthen their credibility. This connection creates a foundation of trust and mutual respect, which is critical for effective teamwork and collaboration. Team members are more likely to go the extra mile when they feel their leader understands and values their efforts.

Credibility also allows leaders to:

> - Navigate Conflict More Effectively: When conflicts arise, your understanding of the team's roles and contributions enables you to mediate fairly and find solutions that consider all perspectives.
> - Gain Honest Feedback: Teams are more likely to provide genuine input when they trust their leader's ability to understand their challenges and act on their concerns.
> - Inspire Innovation: Leaders who connect with their teams create an environment where new ideas are welcomed and supported. Understanding the work being done helps you identify and encourage opportunities for growth and improvement.

1.3. Case Study 1: Understanding Your Team's Work for Better Leadership

The Scenario

James, a newly appointed production manager in a medium-sized manufacturing company, faced the challenge of leading a diverse team of 25 employees, ranging from seasoned machinists to recent engineering graduates. Although James possessed exceptional technical expertise and strategic acumen, he quickly realized that his ability to drive success hinged on understanding the unique strengths, weaknesses, and personalities of his team members.

James noticed that some employees consistently delivered high-quality results, while others struggled to meet deadlines or required constant supervision. Initially, he relied on performance metrics and formal evaluations to gauge his team's abilities. However, the data only revealed part of the picture—numbers showed results, but they didn't explain motivations, challenges, or untapped potential.

The Approach

Recognizing the need for a more personalized approach, James decided to spend time getting to know his team members individually. He adopted the following strategies:

1. One-on-One Conversations:
   James scheduled informal, one-on-one meetings with each team member. Instead of solely focusing on work performance, he asked open-ended questions, such as:
   - "What aspects of your role do you enjoy most?"
   - "Are there any skills or areas you'd like to develop further?"
   - "What challenges do you encounter in your day-to-day work?"
   - "What motivates you to do your best work?"
   - "Is there something you think the team, or I, could do differently to make your work more efficient or fulfilling?"
2. Observing and Listening:
   James spent time on the production floor, observing workflows and informally chatting with team members. He listened carefully to how they spoke about their tasks and challenges, noting recurring themes such as limited training on new

machinery or a lack of communication between shifts.
3. Leveraging Personality Insights:
James paid attention to each team member's personality traits—how they preferred to communicate, whether they thrived in collaborative or independent work, and how they responded to feedback. For example, he discovered that one of his machinists, Sam, was highly detail-oriented but hesitant to share ideas in team meetings. By encouraging Sam privately, James unlocked valuable suggestions for process improvements.

The Results

James' efforts brought tangible benefits to both his team members and himself:

- For the Team Members:
    - Employees felt valued and respected, leading to higher engagement and morale.
    - Team members became more open about their challenges and aspirations, enabling James to tailor his support to individual needs.
    - With James' encouragement, employees gained confidence in their abilities, and several volunteered for additional responsibilities or training opportunities.
- For James as a Leader:
    - By understanding the team's strengths and weaknesses, James could delegate tasks

more effectively, ensuring that the right person handled each job.
- Through the insights gained, James identified gaps in his own technical knowledge and took steps to upskill himself, attending hands-on workshops on the latest production technology.
- The strong relationships James built with his team fostered trust, making it easier to implement changes and resolve conflicts collaboratively.

Open-Ended Questions for Deeper Insights

Here are some examples of open-ended questions James used to understand his team better:

- Performance and Strengths:
    - "What do you think is your biggest strength in your current role?"
    - "Is there a particular project or task where you felt you excelled? What made it successful?"
- Challenges and Weaknesses:
    - "What's the most challenging part of your job, and how do you usually deal with it?"
    - "Are there tools, resources, or training that you think would help you perform better?"
- Personality and Preferences:
    - "Do you prefer working independently or as part of a team? Why?"
    - "How do you like to receive feedback—immediately, during regular reviews, or in another way?"

Lessons Learned

This case demonstrates the profound impact of understanding individual team members on both leadership success and team performance:

- ➤ Building Rapport: James' genuine interest in his team's experiences created a positive environment where employees felt comfortable sharing ideas and concerns.
- ➤ Enhancing Leadership: By leveraging team strengths and addressing weaknesses, James not only improved team efficiency but also became a more effective and empathetic leader.
- ➤ Unlocking Potential: Understanding individual personalities allowed James to align employees' roles with their strengths, paving the way for personal and professional growth.

1.4. Case Study 2: Empowering Teams Through Awareness and Collaboration

When Sarah took on the role of plant manager at a mid-sized manufacturing company specializing in precision automotive components, she knew she was stepping into a complex environment. The company had a reputation for high-quality products but was struggling to meet production deadlines. The delays were threatening to erode customer trust, and it was clear that action was needed.

Sarah had a strong technical background in mechanical engineering and had previously managed smaller teams. However, this was her first time overseeing a large-scale operation with multiple departments and a seasoned workforce. As she walked the factory floor on her first day, she could sense a mix of skepticism and wariness among the employees. Many of them had been with the company for decades and were proud of their expertise. Sarah realized she would need to tread carefully to understand the challenges without undermining their experience.

The Challenge

The main issue was inefficiency in the assembly line, which was causing delays in production schedules. Sarah wanted to identify the root cause of the problem, but she also knew that diving in too aggressively or micromanaging could alienate her team. How could she gain the insights she needed without disrupting the delicate balance of trust and respect?

Sarah's Approach

Instead of immediately making changes or holding a top-down meeting, Sarah chose to take a collaborative and observant approach.

1. Listening and Learning
   Sarah started by spending time on the assembly line, observing workflows and processes. She avoided interrupting or offering suggestions but made herself approachable by greeting employees and asking casual, non-invasive questions. For example, instead of asking, "Why isn't this working?" she would ask, "What do you think slows things down the most?"

This method allowed her to gather valuable insights while demonstrating respect for the team's expertise. Employees began to share their frustrations, such as outdated equipment and a lack of coordination between departments, in an open and constructive manner.

2. Facilitating Ownership
   After gaining an understanding of the issues, Sarah organized a brainstorming session with representatives from the production, maintenance, and logistics teams. She framed the discussion around empowering them to identify solutions, rather than dictating changes.

   "You're the ones who know this process best," she told the group. "What ideas do you have for making it smoother and faster?"

   The team responded enthusiastically, proposing several actionable solutions, including better scheduling practices, clearer communication channels, and upgrading a specific piece of machinery that frequently broke down.

3. Balancing Engagement and Delegation
   While Sarah stayed involved in implementing the changes, she made a conscious effort to delegate responsibilities. For instance, she asked the maintenance team to research machinery upgrades and empowered the logistics team to redesign the scheduling system. This approach gave the employees a sense of ownership and accountability for the improvements.

The Results

Within three months, the assembly line's efficiency improved significantly. The updated scheduling system reduced delays, and the upgraded machinery eliminated frequent breakdowns. Employees reported feeling more engaged and respected, as their ideas had been valued and implemented.

Most importantly, Sarah's leadership style earned her the trust of her team. By taking the time to understand the technical and operational challenges without overstepping, she demonstrated that she was not just a manager but also a partner in their success.

Lessons for Leaders

Sarah's story highlights several critical principles of industrial leadership:

- Awareness Builds Credibility: Spending time understanding workflows and challenges allows leaders to make informed decisions that are grounded in the realities of their team's work. This ensures that decisions are both practical and impactful.
- Empowerment Drives Engagement: When leaders involve employees in problem-solving, they foster a sense of ownership and accountability, leading to better implementation of decisions.
- Balance Is Key: Effective leaders stay informed without micromanaging, finding ways to support their teams while respecting their expertise. This

balance allows for clearer, more strategic decision-making.
- Data-Informed Decision-Making: Observing processes and gathering input from the team provides leaders with a wealth of information to base their decisions on. This ensures that solutions are not only well-informed but also align with both team capabilities and organizational goals.

Questions for Reflection

1. How can leaders strike the right balance between staying informed and micromanaging?
2. What steps can leaders take to create an environment where employees feel comfortable sharing challenges and proposing solutions?
3. How can operational knowledge help leaders align technical improvements with strategic goals?

Chapter 2: Unlocking Team Potential

In the dynamic landscape of industrial operations, success is often determined not just by technology or processes, but by the potential and performance of the people driving them. The role of a leader extends beyond managing day-to-day activities; it involves unlocking the latent potential within a team, guiding individuals to excel, and aligning their collective efforts with the organization's goals.

Every team comprises a unique mix of individuals, each bringing distinct skills, experiences, and perspectives. Recognizing and harnessing this diversity is a hallmark of effective leadership. However, this requires more than a superficial understanding of roles and responsibilities. Leaders must delve deeper, developing a nuanced appreciation of each team member's strengths, identifying areas for growth, and fostering an environment where everyone can thrive. This approach not only enhances individual performance but also builds a cohesive and resilient team capable of tackling challenges and seizing opportunities.

Unlocking team potential begins with assessing the skills and capabilities present within the group. This goes beyond job titles or formal qualifications; it involves understanding how each individual contributes to the team's dynamics and how their unique strengths can be leveraged to achieve common objectives. For instance, one team member might excel at technical problem-solving, while another shines in communication and collaboration. Recognizing these traits allows a leader to assign tasks strategically, ensuring that each person is positioned to succeed while contributing to the team's overall efficiency.

At the same time, leaders must identify areas where development is needed. Growth is an integral part of both individual and organizational success, and addressing skill gaps is crucial for long-term performance. A proactive leader views these gaps not as liabilities but as opportunities for improvement. By investing in training, mentoring, and professional development, leaders empower their teams to adapt to changing demands and excel in their roles. This focus on growth cultivates a culture of continuous learning, which is vital in industries where innovation and agility are key to maintaining a competitive edge.

Another critical aspect of unlocking team potential lies in aligning individual capabilities with organizational goals. When team members understand how their efforts contribute to the broader mission, they are more likely to feel engaged and motivated. This alignment fosters a sense of purpose, turning routine tasks into meaningful contributions. Leaders play a pivotal role in bridging the gap between strategy and execution, ensuring that each team member sees the value of their work within the larger context of the organization's vision.

However, achieving this alignment is not without its challenges. Leaders must balance organizational priorities with individual aspirations, ensuring that goals are not only met but also mutually beneficial. Open communication and active listening are essential in this process. By understanding what drives each team member and addressing their concerns, leaders can create a shared sense of commitment and direction.

Ultimately, unlocking team potential requires a leader to inspire, support, and challenge their team in equal measure. It involves creating an environment where strengths are celebrated, growth is encouraged, and everyone feels valued and empowered to contribute their best. This chapter will explore the strategies and practices that enable leaders to assess their team's capabilities effectively, identify opportunities for development, and align individual efforts with organizational success.

2.1. Assessing Strengths, Skills, and Growth Areas

Every team is built on a foundation of individual strengths, diverse skills, and untapped potential. A leader's ability to assess and understand these elements is critical to fostering a high-performing and adaptable team. While chapter 1 emphasized understanding team members' strengths and weaknesses to build a cohesive foundation, this subchapter delves into the practical process of assessing those strengths, identifying areas for improvement, and creating a pathway for growth that aligns with organizational goals. In an industrial environment, where precision, efficiency, and innovation are essential, this assessment process becomes even more significant.

The Importance of Knowing Your Team's Strengths

Each team member brings something valuable to the table, whether it's technical expertise, problem-solving skills, or leadership potential. Identifying and acknowledging these strengths builds a strong foundation for team dynamics and ensures that individuals feel valued for their contributions. When team members' strengths are recognized, they are more likely to feel motivated and engaged in their work. This is especially important in industrial settings, where tasks are often highly specialized, and recognizing unique expertise can lead to better collaboration and efficiency.

For example, a technician with a knack for troubleshooting complex machinery can become an invaluable resource during critical operations. Similarly, a team member who excels in communication might naturally take on the role of coordinating between different departments. As a leader, your role is to identify these capabilities and ensure they are leveraged effectively.

Recognizing strengths also helps leaders delegate tasks more strategically. When individuals are assigned responsibilities that align with their natural talents, productivity increases, and the team operates more cohesively. Leaders who take the time to understand these dynamics not only improve performance but also create a culture of trust and appreciation.

Assessing Skills for Current and Future Needs

Industrial environments are constantly evolving, with new technologies, processes, and demands emerging regularly. To keep pace, leaders must assess not only the current skills within their teams but also anticipate future needs. This requires a proactive approach to understanding the skill sets of each team member and identifying gaps that may hinder progress.

One effective way to assess skills is through performance evaluations and hands-on observation. By observing how team members handle their day-to-day responsibilities, leaders can gain insights into their technical abilities, problem-solving approaches, and adaptability. Regular one-on-one discussions are also invaluable for understanding employees' perspectives on their own strengths and areas for growth.

A forward-thinking leader will also consider industry trends when assessing skills. For example, if automation or advanced analytics is becoming more prevalent in your sector, it's essential to identify team members who show potential for upskilling in these areas. By aligning assessments with both current and future demands, leaders can ensure their teams remain competitive and prepared for change.

Identifying Growth Areas

While strengths are the foundation of a team's success, growth areas—or opportunities for improvement—are where transformative progress occurs. Identifying these areas requires a careful balance of constructive feedback and encouragement. It's not about pointing out flaws but rather highlighting opportunities to expand skills and achieve greater potential.

Growth areas might include technical capabilities, such as mastering a new piece of machinery, or softer skills, like improving collaboration or time management. Leaders should approach this process with empathy and a growth mindset, emphasizing that improvement is a natural and necessary part of professional development.

To identify growth areas effectively, leaders can:

- Analyze Performance Data: Use metrics and key performance indicators (KPIs) to pinpoint areas where individuals or the team may be falling short. For instance, if error rates are high in a specific process, it could indicate the need for additional training.
- Solicit Feedback: Encourage team members to share their thoughts on what they find challenging and where they'd like to improve. This creates a collaborative approach to development.
- Observe Interactions: Pay attention to how team members interact with one another and with their tasks. Are there patterns of miscommunication or inefficiencies that could be addressed through targeted growth initiatives?

Identifying growth areas also involves understanding the root causes of any challenges. For example, if a team member struggles with meeting deadlines, is it due to a lack of time management skills, or are there external factors, such as unclear expectations or resource limitations, contributing to the issue? Addressing these underlying factors is key to meaningful improvement.

Tools and Strategies for Assessment

Leaders in industrial settings have access to a variety of tools and strategies to assess strengths, skills, and growth areas effectively. Some of these include:

- Skill Matrices: A visual tool that maps out the skills present within a team and identifies gaps. This is

> particularly useful in complex environments where cross-training may be necessary.
> - Competency Frameworks: These frameworks define the specific skills and behaviors required for success in different roles, providing a benchmark for assessment.
> - Feedback Mechanisms: Regular feedback sessions, 360-degree reviews, and peer assessments can offer valuable insights into both strengths and areas for improvement.

By leveraging these tools, leaders can create a clear and actionable picture of their team's capabilities, enabling them to make informed decisions about training, development, and resource allocation.

Encouraging Self-Assessment and Ownership

While a leader's perspective is invaluable, encouraging team members to engage in self-assessment can enhance the process. When individuals take ownership of their development, they are more likely to stay motivated and committed to growth. Leaders can facilitate this by providing self-assessment tools, offering guidance on setting personal goals, and fostering a culture of open dialogue about strengths and improvement areas.

For instance, regular check-ins where team members reflect on their recent performance and set goals for the next period can be highly effective. These conversations not only help individuals stay on track but also provide leaders with deeper insights into their team's aspirations and challenges.

Building a Culture of Growth and Development

Ultimately, assessing strengths, skills, and growth areas is not a one-time exercise but an ongoing process that should be embedded into the team's culture. Leaders who prioritize development and provide consistent opportunities for learning create an environment where everyone feels empowered to contribute their best. This culture of growth benefits not only the individuals and the team but also the organization as a whole, driving innovation and long-term success.

2.2. Aligning Individual Capabilities with Organizational Goals

The Critical Role of Alignment in Industrial Success

In industrial environments, alignment between individual capabilities and organizational goals is more than a managerial ideal—it is a fundamental necessity. The intricate operations of factories, supply chains, and technical teams require seamless coordination, and this cannot be achieved without ensuring that each team member's contributions are in sync with the organization's broader objectives. Misalignment can lead to inefficiencies, communication breakdowns, and diminished morale, ultimately impacting the bottom line.

Successful alignment benefits both parties. For the organization, it drives productivity, innovation, and competitive advantage. For team members, it provides clarity, purpose, and opportunities for meaningful contribution. When individuals understand how their specific roles and skills contribute to the organization's mission, they feel a stronger sense of belonging and are more motivated to excel in their positions.

Understanding Organizational Goals

Before leaders can align team capabilities with organizational objectives, they must first ensure a clear understanding of these goals at all levels. Industrial goals often include improving efficiency, reducing waste, optimizing production, and fostering innovation. These goals are tied to broader strategic aims, such as gaining market share, meeting customer demands, or adhering to sustainability standards.

Leaders should communicate these objectives clearly and consistently. For example, if a manufacturing plant aims to reduce energy consumption by 15% over the next year, team members need to know not only the target but also how their daily actions, such as machine operations or maintenance schedules, contribute to achieving it.

Mapping Capabilities to Goals

Once organizational goals are well-defined and understood, the next step is to map individual capabilities to these objectives. This involves assessing the current skill sets, expertise, and potential of each team member and identifying how their strengths can support the organization's mission.

Steps to Map Capabilities to Goals:

1. Perform Capability Audits: Leaders should use tools like skill matrices or competency frameworks to

evaluate the team's existing capabilities. This process involves identifying technical skills, certifications, problem-solving abilities, and soft skills such as leadership or adaptability.
2. Identify Gaps and Opportunities: After assessing capabilities, leaders should pinpoint gaps that could hinder progress toward organizational goals. For instance, if the organization is transitioning to digital manufacturing, a lack of expertise in data analytics may emerge as a key area for improvement.
3. Create Role-Specific Objectives: Customize roles and responsibilities to align individual strengths with organizational priorities. For example, if an employee demonstrates excellent troubleshooting skills, they could be assigned to lead efforts in minimizing equipment downtime.

The Role of Open Communication

Alignment cannot happen without open and ongoing communication between leaders and their teams. Leaders should actively engage team members in conversations about their aspirations, challenges, and how their work connects to the organization's larger goals. This fosters a shared sense of ownership and accountability.

Tactics for Effective Communication:

- One-on-One Meetings: Regular check-ins provide a platform for discussing personal goals, performance, and alignment with team objectives.

- Team Discussions: Group sessions allow for brainstorming and collaborative goal-setting, ensuring alignment at the team level.
- Transparent Reporting: Sharing updates on organizational progress and how individual contributions have made an impact reinforces the connection between personal effort and collective success.

Leveraging Strengths to Meet Goals

Leaders should aim to maximize each team member's strengths in ways that contribute directly to organizational priorities. This involves rethinking traditional roles and exploring creative ways to deploy talent.

For example, a technically skilled worker who excels in training others could transition into a mentorship role, guiding newer employees while supporting the organization's goal of improving workforce efficiency. Similarly, a leader who recognizes a team member's knack for process optimization might involve them in special projects focused on reducing waste or enhancing productivity.

Navigating Challenges in Alignment

Aligning individual capabilities with organizational goals is not without its challenges. These may include resistance to change, unclear priorities, or skill mismatches. Leaders must approach these obstacles with empathy and adaptability.

Strategies to Overcome Challenges:

- Empower Employees with Training: Offering upskilling opportunities ensures that team members are equipped to meet new challenges and align with evolving goals.
- Clarify Expectations: Vague or conflicting expectations can lead to misalignment. Leaders should articulate clear, measurable objectives for both individuals and teams.
- Foster a Growth Mindset: Encourage employees to view challenges as opportunities for development, helping them adapt to new roles or responsibilities.

Aligning Individual Aspirations with Organizational Success

True alignment occurs when team members feel that their personal and professional aspirations are compatible with the organization's goals. Leaders play a crucial role in bridging these two areas by fostering a culture of mutual respect and shared purpose.

Ways to Bridge Aspirations and Goals:

1. Offer Career Development Opportunities: Employees who see a clear path for growth within the organization are more likely to stay motivated and aligned.
2. Encourage Employee Feedback: Actively seek input from team members on how they envision their roles contributing to organizational success.
3. Recognize and Reward Contributions: Celebrating achievements reinforces positive behaviors and

highlights the connection between individual efforts and organizational outcomes.

Measuring Alignment Success

The success of alignment efforts should be regularly evaluated through metrics and qualitative feedback. Key performance indicators (KPIs) such as productivity rates, employee engagement scores, and goal completion rates can provide insights into how well individual capabilities are aligning with organizational objectives.

Leaders should also prioritize gathering anecdotal feedback from employees and teams. Are team members feeling motivated and connected to the mission? Are they clear about their roles and responsibilities? These qualitative insights are just as important as hard data in gauging alignment.

2.3. Case Study 1: Assessing Strengths, Skills, and Growth Areas in an Industrial Team

Background: The Precision Manufacturing Facility
PrecisionTechX Industries is a mid-sized manufacturing company specializing in precision-engineered components for the aerospace sector. With tight production timelines and a zero-tolerance policy for defects, the company operates in a high-stakes environment. Its success depends on a skilled and adaptable workforce capable of navigating complex technical challenges.

The leadership team at PrecisionTechX recognizes that their competitive edge lies not only in advanced machinery but also in the capabilities of their workforce. However, a recent review of production timelines revealed delays and inconsistent quality metrics. The CEO tasked the plant manager, Anna, with diagnosing and resolving the issues by focusing on assessing the strengths, skills, and growth areas of her 50-member team.

Initial Challenges and Observations
Anna identified several challenges during her initial assessment:

1. Unclear Strengths: While team members were experienced, their specific strengths were not well-documented. For example, a machinist with years of experience might have advanced troubleshooting skills, but these were neither leveraged nor recognized formally.
2. Outdated Skills: The industry had recently adopted new computer numerical control (CNC) software, but only 20% of the team was proficient in its use.
3. Unidentified Growth Areas: Anna suspected that some inefficiencies were due to unaddressed skill gaps but lacked concrete data to pinpoint these areas.
4. Morale and Engagement: Team members felt their contributions were undervalued, and some believed that their career progression opportunities were limited.

Strategy for Assessing Strengths, Skills, and Growth Areas
Anna implemented a structured, multi-phase approach to address these challenges:

Phase 1: Data Collection

1. Skill Matrix Development: Anna developed a detailed skill matrix that included technical proficiencies, problem-solving capabilities, leadership potential, and adaptability.
2. Surveys and Self-Assessments: Each team member completed a confidential self-assessment survey where they rated their comfort level with various tasks and identified areas where they sought improvement.
3. One-on-One Interviews: Anna scheduled short but focused interviews with every team member to discuss their work, aspirations, and perceived strengths. These conversations uncovered hidden talents and aspirations.

For example, one employee, Alan, revealed a deep interest in robotics programming, an area not currently utilized in his role but highly relevant to the company's future projects.

Phase 2: Observational Analysis

Anna spent several days observing the team during production runs and meetings. She paid close attention to:

- Task Efficiency: Noting which employees excelled in specific processes.
- Problem-Solving: Identifying who took initiative when unexpected challenges arose.
- Collaboration: Assessing team dynamics and how individuals communicated and supported each other.

Phase 3: External Validation

To complement her internal findings, Anna brought in an external consultant to conduct a technical assessment of the team's CNC programming capabilities. This unbiased evaluation provided a baseline for training initiatives.

Results of the Assessment
The assessment yielded actionable insights:

1. Documented Strengths: Anna discovered that 10 team members excelled in process optimization, while others showed natural leadership abilities or expertise in quality control.
2. Skill Gaps: The evaluation highlighted a need for immediate training in CNC software and advanced troubleshooting techniques.
3. Potential Leaders: Two employees demonstrated exceptional team coordination skills, marking them as candidates for supervisory roles.
4. Growth Aspirations: Several team members expressed interest in cross-training for roles in quality assurance and logistics.

Implementation of Findings
With the data in hand, Anna implemented several initiatives:

1. Targeted Training Programs: She partnered with a local technical institute to provide CNC training for the entire team. Advanced courses were offered to employees showing potential in robotics and programming.

2. Cross-Training Opportunities: Employees interested in expanding their skill sets were paired with mentors from other departments.
3. Recognition Programs: Anna introduced a monthly "Skill Spotlight" where employees' unique contributions were celebrated during team meetings.
4. Leadership Development: The two identified leadership candidates were enrolled in a supervisory training program to prepare them for future roles.

Challenges and Adjustments

Initially, some team members were resistant to the new initiatives, citing time constraints and skepticism about the outcomes. Anna addressed these concerns by:

- Offering Flexible Training Schedules: Classes were arranged during off-peak hours to avoid disrupting production.
- Communicating the Vision: Anna held a town hall meeting to explain how these changes would benefit both the team and the company.

Outcomes and Benefits

After six months, PrecisionTechX saw significant improvements:

1. Enhanced Efficiency: Downtime during production runs decreased by 25%, thanks to the team's improved proficiency in CNC operations.
2. Increased Morale: Employees reported feeling more valued and confident in their roles, leading to

a 30% improvement in employee engagement scores.
3. Improved Retention: Turnover rates dropped as employees saw clear opportunities for growth and development.
4. Operational Resilience: Cross-training efforts ensured that critical tasks were never dependent on a single individual, enhancing overall team adaptability.

Lessons Learned

1. The Importance of Documentation: Maintaining a clear, updated record of team members' skills is invaluable for making informed decisions.
2. The Power of Personalization: Tailored development plans resonate more with employees than generic solutions.
3. Open Communication Is Key: Building trust and buy-in from the team requires transparent and consistent dialogue.
4. Assessment Is an Ongoing Process: Regular evaluations ensure that the team remains aligned with evolving organizational needs.

2.4. Case Study 2: Aligning Individual Capabilities with Organizational Goals

Background: Renewable Energy Operations
GreenXYZ Energy is a leading renewable energy company specializing in the construction and maintenance of solar farms. The company prides itself on innovation and sustainability, striving to stay at the forefront of an industry experiencing rapid growth and transformation.

However, recent feedback from project managers revealed that many team members were unclear about how their day-to-day roles contributed to the company's broader mission. This misalignment was causing inefficiencies, lowered motivation, and missed opportunities for operational excellence.

The leadership team, spearheaded by operations director Matthew, recognized the need to bridge this gap. They set out to better align the unique capabilities of their workforce with the organization's strategic goals, ensuring that every team member felt connected to the company's vision while maximizing their contributions.

The Challenges

1. Disconnected Roles: Technicians and administrative staff often worked in silos, unaware of how their tasks influenced each other or the larger company objectives.
2. Underutilized Skills: Some employees possessed advanced skills that were not being used effectively in their current roles.
3. Lack of Clarity: Many team members lacked a clear understanding of the company's long-term goals, leading to a focus on immediate tasks rather than strategic outcomes.

Strategy for Aligning Capabilities with Goals

Step 1: Defining Organizational Goals

Before aligning individual capabilities, Matthew and his leadership team revisited the company's strategic objectives. They identified three key focus areas for the upcoming year:

1. Expansion into New Markets: Building solar farms in underserved regions.
2. Technological Leadership: Incorporating cutting-edge energy storage solutions.
3. Community Engagement: Increasing visibility and impact in local communities.

With these goals defined, the leadership team analyzed how each department and role could contribute to achieving them.

Step 2: Conducting Individual Capability Assessments

To understand the potential within the workforce, Matthew's team used a combination of methods:

1. Employee Surveys: Focused on understanding personal career goals, skills, and interests.
2. Task Audits: Analyzed how employees spent their time and whether their efforts aligned with strategic priorities.
3. Leadership Feedback: Gathered input from managers about employees' hidden talents and areas of underperformance.

Through this process, the team uncovered valuable insights. For instance, Emma, an administrative assistant, had a background in community outreach and marketing—a skill set highly relevant to GreenXYZ's goal of increasing local engagement. Meanwhile, David, a field technician, demonstrated a knack for analyzing data from solar panels, an ability crucial for optimizing energy storage solutions.

Step 3: Creating Alignment Plans

The leadership team developed a tailored alignment plan for each department, incorporating:

1. Role Redefinition: Adjusting job descriptions to better reflect strategic priorities.
2. Skill Utilization: Reassigning tasks to capitalize on underused skills.
3. Goal Integration: Introducing regular briefings to show how daily tasks connected to the broader company mission.

For example, Emma transitioned into a hybrid role that combined her administrative duties with managing community outreach initiatives. David began collaborating with the R&D team to refine data analytics processes for solar panel performance.

Step 4: Communication and Training

To ensure buy-in, Matthew conducted company-wide sessions explaining the alignment process. These sessions emphasized:

- The "Why": How each person's role impacted GreenWave's success.
- The "How": Clear, actionable steps for aligning individual efforts with company goals.
- Support Systems: Training opportunities to address any skill gaps that emerged during realignment.

Employees were encouraged to share feedback and suggest improvements, fostering a sense of collaboration and ownership.

Results and Impact

After six months of implementing the alignment strategy, GreenWave saw measurable improvements:

1. Increased Efficiency: Employees spent 20% less time on redundant tasks, allowing more focus on strategic projects.
2. Improved Engagement: Surveys showed a 40% increase in employees feeling "highly connected" to the company's mission.
3. Enhanced Innovation: With David's data analytics skills in use, the company optimized energy storage efficiency by 15%, setting a new industry benchmark.
4. Community Impact: Emma's outreach initiatives led to partnerships with three local schools, boosting GreenWave's reputation in target regions.

Overcoming Challenges
Not everything went smoothly. Initial resistance emerged from employees who were concerned about additional responsibilities. To address this, Matthew:

- Ensured Proper Training: Employees stepping into new roles received hands-on support and resources.
- Provided Clear Communication: Regular updates helped manage expectations and highlight early successes.

- Recognized Achievements: Public acknowledgment of contributions motivated others to embrace the changes.

Lessons Learned

1. Customization Matters: A one-size-fits-all approach doesn't work. Tailored alignment plans yield better results.
2. Leadership Engagement: Visible, consistent involvement from leaders builds trust and momentum.
3. Adaptability Is Key: Continual reassessment ensures that alignment efforts stay relevant as organizational goals evolve.
4. Clarity Drives Connection: When employees see the direct impact of their work, they are more engaged and motivated.

Chapter 3: Humanizing Leadership: Building Bridges Beyond the Workplace

Leadership in the modern industrial landscape extends far beyond project deadlines, productivity targets, and technical expertise. While metrics and goals are critical for organizational success, they only tell part of the story. At its heart, exceptional leadership is rooted in relationships—genuine, meaningful connections that go beyond professional roles and responsibilities. Leaders who understand the human side of their teams are better equipped to inspire loyalty, foster collaboration, and create a culture where individuals thrive.

In today's fast-paced, results-driven work environments, it's easy to focus solely on outputs and overlook the individuals driving them. Yet, teams are more than the sum of their tasks; they are collections of people with diverse experiences, motivations, and aspirations. Recognizing this complexity is not just a compassionate gesture—it's a strategic advantage. By understanding employees as multidimensional individuals rather than merely contributors to business goals, leaders can unlock unparalleled levels of engagement, creativity, and commitment.

Humanizing leadership means seeing the people behind the roles, fostering environments where employees feel valued not just for what they do but for who they are. This approach requires leaders to step out of traditional hierarchies and cultivate trust, empathy, and mutual respect. It involves creating spaces where conversations aren't limited to tasks or deadlines but extend to shared experiences, personal challenges, and collective achievements. Whether it's through team-building activities, informal outings, or simply taking the time to celebrate milestones, leaders who prioritize relationships lay the groundwork for stronger, more resilient teams.

One critical aspect of this approach is recognizing that the boundaries between professional and personal lives are increasingly blurred. Employees bring their whole selves to work, and understanding the factors influencing their well-being—both inside and outside the office—enables leaders to provide meaningful support. This support might manifest in flexible work arrangements, opportunities for personal growth, or simply showing empathy during challenging times. When leaders acknowledge and address these dimensions, they not only humanize the workplace but also reinforce the idea that success is a shared journey.

The benefits of building bridges beyond the workplace extend far beyond the immediate team. Human-centered leadership creates a ripple effect that strengthens organizational culture, attracts top talent, and builds lasting loyalty. It also challenges conventional leadership paradigms, replacing rigid, top-down models with collaborative, inclusive approaches that reflect the values and aspirations of modern workplaces.

This chapter delves into practical strategies for humanizing leadership and building bridges that connect people beyond the confines of their roles. It will explore how team outings, shared experiences, and an emphasis on personal connections can transform the workplace into a hub of collaboration and innovation. By fostering relationships that transcend the workplace, leaders can not only achieve remarkable results but also leave a lasting impact on the lives they touch.

3.1. Why Team Building Matters

Leadership today is not just about meeting targets or executing strategies—it's about creating environments where individuals feel valued, connected, and empowered to contribute their best. Team building plays a critical role in achieving this by fostering bonds that transcend workplace hierarchies and job descriptions. When leaders invest time and effort into building connections, they set the stage for collaboration, trust, and resilience.

One of the most significant psychological benefits of team building is its ability to promote a sense of belonging. In any organization, feeling included and appreciated boosts morale and reduces stress. This sense of inclusion becomes a powerful driver of performance and innovation. Through team-building activities, employees can interact with colleagues in ways that go beyond their professional personas. These interactions help humanize relationships, breaking down barriers and fostering empathy.

For example, when teams engage in activities outside the workplace—be it a casual lunch or an adventurous ropes course—they tap into different facets of their personalities. These settings allow individuals to showcase hidden strengths or talents that may not surface in day-to-day work. A reserved employee might demonstrate leadership during a problem-solving game, or an analytical thinker might reveal creativity during a team art project.

Such discoveries can shift workplace dynamics, encouraging colleagues to view each other with renewed respect and appreciation.

Moreover, team building fosters camaraderie, which is essential during challenging times. Shared experiences—especially those that involve fun or adventure—create bonds that make teams more cohesive and resilient. When people know and trust each other on a personal level, they are more likely to support one another in overcoming workplace challenges.

Team building also positively impacts emotional well-being. Casual, non-work-related interactions provide employees with an opportunity to unwind, reducing workplace stress. Laughter, shared memories, and collective achievements create a positive emotional climate that benefits both individuals and the organization.

Finally, team building aligns with a core principle of effective leadership: leading by example. When leaders actively participate in team-building activities, they signal a commitment to relationship-building and personal growth. This involvement strengthens the leader's connection with their team, fostering trust and mutual respect.

3.2. Types of Team Building Activities

Team building comes in many shapes and sizes, each offering unique opportunities for growth, connection, and enjoyment. The most effective activities are those that align with your team's interests, goals, and cultural dynamics. This subchapter explores several categories of team-building activities, providing insights into their benefits and how they can foster stronger, more collaborative teams.

Outdoor Adventures

Outdoor activities provide a refreshing change of pace from the office environment, encouraging trust, collaboration, and problem-solving.

- Hiking: Whether it's a leisurely trail or a challenging climb, hiking offers teams the chance to work together toward a shared goal while enjoying nature. It promotes endurance, teamwork, and communication as members navigate paths and support one another.
- Ropes Courses: These activities are particularly effective for building trust and pushing people out of their comfort zones. From ziplining to trust falls, ropes courses challenge individuals to rely on their teammates, fostering confidence and camaraderie.
- Team Sports: Organized games like soccer, volleyball, or softball allow employees to channel their competitive spirit in a healthy, fun environment. Sports cultivate collaboration, leadership, and mutual encouragement.

Outdoor adventures not only strengthen bonds but also allow participants to engage in physical activity, which has been shown to boost mental clarity and reduce stress.

Skill-Based Workshops

Skill-based workshops combine fun with personal and professional development, offering participants an opportunity to learn while building connections.

- Cooking Classes: Working together to prepare a meal fosters cooperation and creativity. Cooking encourages participants to delegate tasks, experiment, and celebrate the end product as a team.
- Creative Sessions: Activities such as painting, pottery, or music workshops unleash creativity and provide a platform for self-expression. They allow individuals to showcase different talents and appreciate the unique contributions of their teammates.
- Collaborative Art Projects: Projects like mural painting or creating a vision board require collective brainstorming and execution, reinforcing the value of teamwork.

Workshops like these are particularly valuable for breaking down barriers, as they focus on shared learning rather than workplace hierarchies.

Community Service

Volunteering together fosters a sense of purpose and shared values, creating a deeper emotional connection among team members.

- Charity Events: Participating in events such as fundraisers, marathons, or food drives provides a

platform for collective effort toward a greater good.
- ➢ Environmental Initiatives: Activities like beach cleanups or tree planting promote teamwork while reinforcing a sense of environmental stewardship.
- ➢ Helping Local Communities: Partnering with local organizations to support schools, shelters, or underserved populations helps instill a sense of gratitude and social responsibility.

Community service activities enable teams to bond over a shared mission while building a positive image for the organization.

Casual Outings

Sometimes, the simplest activities can have the most profound impact. Casual outings provide an informal setting for employees to relax, connect, and enjoy each other's company.

- ➢ Team Lunches or Dinners: Sharing a meal fosters informal conversation and connection. Celebrating milestones or simply gathering for lunch helps create a sense of community.
- ➢ Coffee Meetups: Regular coffee breaks outside the office encourage casual interaction and give team members an opportunity to discuss ideas in a relaxed setting.
- ➢ Trivia Nights or Game Nights: Lighthearted games stimulate friendly competition and teamwork while creating shared memories.

Casual outings are particularly effective for breaking down silos and encouraging collaboration across departments or teams.

3.3. Fun and Meaningful Examples

When team-building activities are designed with creativity and intentionality, they create lasting impressions and tangible benefits for the group. Below are some examples of leaders who have transformed workplace dynamics through engaging and meaningful team-building exercises, showcasing how innovative approaches can strengthen teams and enhance collaboration.

The Escape Room Challenge

A visionary tech CEO once organized a company-wide escape room challenge to foster strategic thinking and problem-solving. Teams were tasked with solving intricate puzzles, uncovering clues, and unlocking their way out of themed rooms under a time constraint.

Why It Worked:

- ➢ The high-pressure, collaborative environment encouraged team members to think critically and rely on each other's strengths.
- ➢ Leaders observed natural roles emerge—some employees took charge as strategists, while others excelled as detail-oriented analysts or creative problem-solvers.
- ➢ The exercise revealed untapped potential in employees who demonstrated leadership and resourcefulness outside their typical roles.

This activity not only energized the team but also reinforced the importance of cross-functional collaboration and innovative thinking in tackling challenges.

Celebrating Milestones with a Barbecue

In the manufacturing sector, a plant manager named Alex decided to celebrate a major production milestone with a team barbecue. Employees were invited to a local park, where they enjoyed food, games, and casual conversation with colleagues and their families.

Why It Worked:

- The relaxed setting allowed employees to connect on a personal level, breaking down hierarchical barriers.
- Including family members in the celebration created a sense of inclusivity and showed appreciation for the broader support system that contributes to the employees' success.
- It reinforced the company's commitment to recognizing achievements in a meaningful way, boosting morale and loyalty.

The event not only celebrated the team's hard work but also built a sense of pride and unity, encouraging employees to strive for future milestones.

Themed Hackathon Weekends

At an innovative startup, the leadership team organized themed hackathon weekends where employees from different departments collaborated on passion projects. Teams were given the freedom to brainstorm and develop solutions outside their regular job scope, with the best ideas receiving funding for further development.

Why It Worked:

- This initiative empowered employees to unleash their creativity in a supportive and risk-free environment.
- It fostered interdepartmental connections as individuals from engineering, marketing, and customer service came together to tackle challenges.
- The event inspired a culture of innovation, with many projects contributing to real business improvements.

Such hackathons serve as a powerful reminder that leadership includes providing opportunities for employees to showcase their unique ideas and talents.

Volunteering with a Cause

Another example comes from a healthcare company, where the CEO organized a day of volunteering at a local children's hospital. Teams painted murals, assembled care packages, and spent time engaging with patients.

Why It Worked:

- Employees developed a deeper connection by working together toward a meaningful cause.

- The experience instilled a shared sense of purpose that transcended the workplace.
- It highlighted the organization's values, reinforcing employee pride in being part of a company that contributes to the community.

The day fostered team unity while also boosting the company's reputation as a socially responsible organization.

Rotating Cultural Exchange Dinners

A multinational corporation with a diverse workforce introduced a monthly cultural exchange dinner, where employees took turns hosting themed meals that showcased their heritage.

Why It Worked:

- This initiative celebrated diversity and encouraged employees to share personal stories, building empathy and understanding among team members.
- The dinners created a sense of belonging, particularly for employees from underrepresented backgrounds.
- Leaders participated actively, demonstrating their commitment to inclusivity and creating stronger connections with their teams.

This approach not only enriched the company culture but also fostered a global mindset, preparing the team for success in a competitive international market.

3.4. Building Personal Connections

Strong leadership extends beyond the workplace; it is rooted in authentic relationships built on trust and mutual respect. Leaders who invest in getting to know their team members as individuals, not just employees, foster a culture of inclusivity, belonging, and engagement. This subchapter provides actionable tips for leaders to deepen personal connections with their teams, enhancing both morale and productivity.

Understanding Hobbies, Family, and Aspirations

One of the simplest yet most impactful ways to connect with team members is by taking a genuine interest in their lives beyond work. Asking thoughtful questions about hobbies, family, or future goals (in appropriate and respectful settings) shows employees that their leader values them as whole individuals.

Practical Tips for Leaders:

- During casual conversations, ask open-ended questions like, "What do you enjoy doing outside of work?" or "Is there a skill you've always wanted to learn?"
- Share your own interests or stories, creating a reciprocal dynamic that invites open communication.
- Pay attention to the small details—mentioning a hobby or interest they've previously shared shows attentiveness and care.

By fostering these conversations, leaders can uncover hidden talents, align work opportunities with personal aspirations, and create an environment of mutual appreciation.

Celebrating Personal Milestones

Recognizing individual milestones such as birthdays, work anniversaries, or personal achievements can have a profound impact on employee morale. These celebrations demonstrate that the organization values its people beyond their professional contributions.

Ideas for Meaningful Recognition:

- Host a small, informal team gathering to celebrate birthdays or significant personal achievements, such as completing a marathon or earning a certification.
- Send personalized notes or emails of congratulations, highlighting the individual's contribution to the team.
- Consider thoughtful but simple gestures, like a card signed by the entire team or a small gift that aligns with their interests.

Such recognition reinforces the idea that employees are seen, appreciated, and supported, contributing to a sense of belonging.

Creating Inclusive Spaces

For personal connections to flourish, leaders must actively cultivate an inclusive environment where every team member feels valued and respected. Inclusive spaces encourage open dialogue, celebrate diversity, and ensure all voices are heard.

Strategies to Build Inclusivity:

- Establish team rituals, such as morning check-ins or casual end-of-week gatherings, where employees can share updates or reflect on the week.
- Rotate leadership roles during meetings or projects to empower quieter team members and give everyone a chance to contribute.
- Use inclusive language that acknowledges diverse backgrounds, avoiding assumptions about personal lives or experiences.

Inclusive spaces create psychological safety, where employees feel confident expressing their ideas and authentic selves without fear of judgment. This leads to stronger collaboration and a deeper connection to the team.

The Ripple Effect of Personal Connections

When leaders prioritize building personal connections, they create a ripple effect throughout the organization. Teams become more cohesive, communication improves, and employees are more likely to go above and beyond in their roles. These connections also foster resilience, enabling teams to navigate challenges together with mutual trust and support.

By asking meaningful questions, celebrating milestones, and creating inclusive spaces, leaders not only enhance individual relationships but also contribute to a workplace culture where everyone feels seen, valued, and motivated to succeed.

3.5. Balancing Fun and Productivity

Team-building activities are powerful tools to strengthen relationships, foster trust, and enhance collaboration, but their true value lies in their alignment with organizational goals and cultural values. Striking the right balance between fun and productivity ensures that such initiatives serve their intended purpose without feeling forced, frivolous, or exclusionary. This subchapter explores how leaders can design meaningful activities that resonate with diverse team members and support both individual and collective growth.

Fun with a Purpose: Aligning Activities with Organizational Culture

To be effective, team-building activities must reflect and reinforce the values and mission of the organization. Outings or exercises that feel disconnected from workplace priorities may be enjoyable in the moment but fail to produce lasting benefits.

Best Practices for Alignment:

- ➢ Define Objectives: Before planning an activity, determine its goal. Is it to improve communication, encourage creativity, or simply show appreciation for the team's hard work?
- ➢ Incorporate Organizational Themes: For example, a company focused on sustainability might organize

a tree-planting day, while a tech-driven organization could host an innovation hackathon.
- ➢ Link to Everyday Work: Activities that mirror workplace challenges, such as collaborative problem-solving or creative brainstorming, reinforce skills that directly benefit productivity.

By ensuring activities are purposeful and tied to the organization's identity, leaders can create experiences that are not only enjoyable but also impactful.

The Importance of Inclusivity

Diversity in teams brings varied perspectives, skills, and strengths, but it also means team members have different preferences and abilities. A successful team-building initiative considers this diversity and ensures every individual feels included and valued.

Strategies for Inclusivity:

- ➢ Offer Variety: Plan a mix of activities that cater to different interests, from physically active events like hiking to quieter options like trivia nights or creative workshops.
- ➢ Address Accessibility: Ensure activities are accessible to everyone, accounting for physical, sensory, or other individual needs. For instance, virtual escape rooms can offer an engaging alternative to a physical ropes course.
- ➢ Gather Input: Involve the team in planning by soliciting suggestions or conducting a quick poll. This not only increases buy-in but also ensures activities reflect the group's collective preferences.

Inclusivity fosters an environment where everyone feels welcome to participate, deepening the sense of belonging within the team.

Avoiding Overload: The Right Frequency and Approach

While team-building activities are valuable, overdoing them can lead to diminished returns or even fatigue. Striking the right balance requires thoughtful timing and execution.

Tips for Finding the Right Balance:

- Quality Over Quantity: A few well-executed activities throughout the year can be more effective than frequent, poorly planned events.
- Be Mindful of Workload: Avoid scheduling activities during peak work periods or immediately after stressful deadlines.
- Encourage Voluntary Participation: Make it clear that while participation is encouraged, no one should feel pressured to attend.

Balancing frequency and timing ensures that team-building remains a positive experience rather than a source of stress or distraction.

The Dual Benefit: Fun and Productivity Intertwined

When executed thoughtfully, team-building activities contribute to both fun and productivity by strengthening interpersonal bonds, encouraging collaboration, and reinforcing shared values. They provide teams with a chance to recharge and reconnect, improving morale and fostering a sense of unity.

By aligning activities with organizational goals, embracing inclusivity, and respecting individual preferences, leaders can harness the power of team-building to create a workplace culture that thrives on both connection and productivity.

3.6. Unexpected Benefits

Team-building activities are often planned with clear, tangible goals in mind—improving communication, fostering collaboration, or celebrating milestones. However, their true value frequently extends beyond these objectives. Informal and relaxed settings provide opportunities for unexpected and transformative outcomes that can profoundly impact team dynamics, innovation, and organizational resilience.

Sparking Innovation Through Relaxed Brainstorming

The pressure of formal meetings or structured work environments can sometimes stifle creativity. In contrast, informal settings create a space where ideas flow more freely. Without the constraints of hierarchies or time limits, team members feel more empowered to share unconventional thoughts and explore possibilities.

How It Happens:

- ➢ Casual Conversations Lead to Breakthroughs: A simple discussion during a team lunch or a shared

laugh during a trivia night can spark ideas that might not emerge in structured settings.
- Cross-Pollination of Ideas: Informal gatherings encourage interactions between departments or roles that might not regularly collaborate, fostering fresh perspectives and innovative thinking.
- Stress-Free Ideation: In a relaxed environment, team members feel less pressure to "get it right," leading to more open exploration of creative solutions.

Many successful organizations have credited their most innovative ideas to moments of casual, unstructured interaction during team-building activities.

Boosting Resilience During Challenging Times

Difficult periods—whether due to industry disruptions, organizational changes, or external crises—test the strength of teams. Informal team-building activities provide the foundation for collective resilience, helping teams navigate these challenges with confidence and unity.

Key Benefits to Resilience:

- Strengthened Emotional Bonds: Shared experiences outside the workplace create a sense of camaraderie that makes team members more likely to support one another during tough times.
- Reinforced Trust: Trust developed during casual outings or shared problem-solving activities helps teams stay cohesive under pressure.

- Perspective Shifts: Informal settings allow teams to step back from immediate challenges, fostering a sense of optimism and recalibration.

By investing in team-building during stable periods, organizations create a safety net of trust and solidarity that becomes invaluable during times of uncertainty.

Building Lasting Loyalty and Mutual Respect

One of the most significant long-term benefits of team-building activities is the loyalty and mutual respect they foster among team members and between employees and leadership. These outcomes often emerge subtly but have a profound impact on workplace culture.

How It Unfolds:

- Personal Connections Build Loyalty: When team members see each other as individuals beyond their roles—learning about hobbies, families, or personal milestones—they develop a deeper commitment to the team's success.
- Leadership Becomes Relatable: Informal interactions humanize leaders, breaking down barriers and demonstrating that leadership values its people.
- Shared Memories Create Unity: Positive experiences, like solving an escape room challenge or volunteering together, leave lasting impressions that strengthen team identity.

These bonds not only enhance day-to-day collaboration but also make teams more resilient to turnover, disengagement, or external challenges.

Unlocking the Potential of Informal Settings

The unexpected benefits of team-building activities lie in their ability to create a sense of psychological safety, spark creativity, and forge connections that endure beyond the workplace. While their outcomes may not always be immediately measurable, their long-term value becomes evident in the trust, innovation, and resilience they cultivate within teams.

By embracing the potential of informal settings, leaders can unlock a deeper layer of team dynamics, ensuring that their organizations are not only productive but also deeply connected and forward-thinking.

3.7. Leadership in Action: Stories of Impact

Leadership is often best understood through the lens of real-world examples. Stories of leaders who embraced non-traditional approaches to team-building offer valuable insights into how creativity, empathy, and intentionality can transform teams. These examples showcase how unconventional methods can foster unity, spark innovation, and build lasting bonds.

Case Study 1: A Cultural Exchange Event That Strengthened a Global Team

Background:
A multinational tech company faced challenges in uniting

its geographically dispersed teams. With employees spread across continents, cultural differences and time zones often hindered collaboration and led to misunderstandings.

The Leader's Approach:
Recognizing the need for a shared sense of identity, the company's COO initiated a biannual cultural exchange event called "Around the World in a Day." Employees from each region were encouraged to share elements of their culture, such as food, traditions, music, and personal stories, through in-person gatherings or virtual showcases.

Results:

- Enhanced Empathy and Understanding: Team members gained deeper appreciation for their colleagues' cultural backgrounds, reducing biases and fostering mutual respect.
- Stronger Collaboration: The event bridged cultural gaps, improving communication and collaboration across regions.
- Lasting Impact: Employees reported feeling more connected to the organization and motivated to contribute to its global mission.

Case Study 2: Monthly Storytelling Sessions for Team Unity

Background:
At a mid-sized media company, the editorial team struggled with low morale and a sense of disconnect due to the pressures of tight deadlines and competitive industry dynamics.

The Leader's Approach:
The department head introduced monthly storytelling sessions called "Story Circle," where employees were invited to share personal anecdotes or professional challenges they had overcome. These gatherings were informal, held over lunch, and participation was voluntary.

Results:

- Increased Trust: Sharing personal stories created a safe space where team members felt heard and valued, deepening interpersonal connections.
- Shared Learning: Stories of professional challenges often sparked discussions on best practices, leading to process improvements and creative solutions.
- Cultural Shift: Over time, the storytelling sessions fostered a culture of openness, reducing silos and encouraging collaboration across departments.

Case Study 3: A Manufacturing Leader Who Leveraged "Random Pairing Lunches"

Background:
In a manufacturing plant with over 300 employees, silos between departments created inefficiencies and missed opportunities for cross-functional learning.

The Leader's Approach:
The plant manager implemented a "Random Pairing Lunch" program, where employees were paired with someone from a different department for a monthly lunch. Participants were given conversation prompts, such as discussing work challenges or personal interests.

Results:

- ➢ Cross-Department Collaboration: Employees began sharing insights and best practices, leading to improved workflows and innovation.
- ➢ Improved Morale: The informal lunches helped employees feel more connected to the broader organization, boosting engagement and retention.
- ➢ Stronger Leadership Pipeline: Junior employees gained visibility with leadership during these lunches, inspiring them to pursue internal growth opportunities.

Lessons Learned

1. Creativity Breeds Connection: Non-traditional activities, like cultural exchanges and storytelling, create unique opportunities for team members to bond beyond their roles.
2. Leadership's Role in Modeling Openness: Leaders who actively participate in or endorse these activities demonstrate their commitment to fostering a connected, inclusive workplace.
3. Small Actions, Big Impacts: Even simple initiatives, like pairing employees for lunch, can lead to profound improvements in collaboration and morale.

Through these examples, leaders can see the value of thinking outside the box to strengthen their teams, proving that innovative approaches to team-building are not just beneficial but transformative.

Part 2: Driving Change and Growth

"Leaders who dare to disrupt yesterday's norms create tomorrow's opportunities."

Chapter 4: Challenging the Status Quo

In the industrial world, where precision, efficiency, and routine often dictate operations, it can be tempting to rely on established methods and procedures. However, while tradition provides a foundation for stability, it can also become a barrier to progress. Industries evolve rapidly, driven by advancements in technology, changing market demands, and the pursuit of higher efficiency. In such an environment, one of the most critical skills a leader can possess is the ability to challenge the status quo constructively. Effective leadership is not about preserving the past; it's about preparing for the future by questioning, innovating, and adapting.

Challenging the status quo is not simply about making changes for the sake of change. It requires a thoughtful approach that respects the knowledge and experience embedded in existing processes while seeking opportunities for improvement. Leaders must cultivate an open-minded perspective and encourage their teams to do the same, transforming skepticism into curiosity and resistance into collaboration. By questioning "how it's always been done," leaders can uncover inefficiencies, identify emerging opportunities, and inspire a culture of continuous innovation.

This chapter explores the delicate balance between honoring the expertise built over years of experience and fostering an environment that embraces new ideas. It delves into how leaders can create a culture where innovation thrives, risks are evaluated strategically, and adaptability becomes a competitive advantage. The journey to challenging the status quo is one of curiosity, resilience, and leadership at its most transformative.

4.1. Rethinking "How It's Always Been Done": The Leader's Role in Questioning Norms

In the dynamic world of industry, the phrase "how it's always been done" often signals a deep-seated adherence to routine and tradition. While tradition can provide stability, it can also become a barrier to innovation, preventing organizations from adapting to evolving demands, technologies, and market expectations. As leaders, embracing the role of a thoughtful challenger is vital for fostering growth, ensuring long-term success, and staying competitive.

Why Questioning Entrenched Practices is Vital for Growth

Industries evolve at an unprecedented pace, with technological advancements, global market shifts, and changing workforce dynamics necessitating constant adaptation. Leaders who resist questioning entrenched practices risk stagnation, inefficiency, and obsolescence. Tradition, while often rooted in past success, may fail to address the complexities of the present or the needs of the future. By questioning "how it's always been done," leaders open the door to identifying inefficiencies, embracing emerging opportunities, and positioning their organizations for sustainable growth.

For example, a manufacturing company clinging to manual processes despite the availability of automation may struggle to meet production demands or remain cost-competitive. By examining these practices and seeking alternatives, leaders can uncover opportunities to enhance productivity and quality while reducing costs. This mindset benefits not only the organization but also employees, as outdated practices often contribute to workplace frustrations or inefficiencies.

Strategies for Respectfully Challenging Outdated Systems

Challenging entrenched norms can be a delicate process. Leaders must navigate the tension between driving change and respecting the expertise and experience of their teams. The following strategies provide a roadmap for questioning norms in a way that inspires collaboration and minimizes resistance:

1. Build a Case for Change
   Before advocating for change, gather evidence to illustrate why existing practices may no longer be effective. Use data, case studies, or comparisons with industry standards to provide a clear, compelling rationale. For instance, if a production method is causing bottlenecks, presenting metrics that highlight inefficiencies can foster understanding and buy-in.

2. Engage Key Stakeholders
   Involve team members, particularly those directly impacted by the practice in question, early in the process. This inclusive approach not only demonstrates respect for their insights but also helps identify potential challenges or resistance

points. Open discussions can also surface alternative solutions that may not have been considered otherwise.

3. Frame the Conversation Positively
   Position change as an opportunity rather than a critique of past methods. Emphasize the potential benefits, such as improved efficiency, reduced workload, or enhanced safety. Acknowledge the value of the existing practice, recognizing its past contributions, before transitioning to the proposed improvements.

4. Pilot and Iterate
   Instead of implementing sweeping changes all at once, consider piloting a new approach on a small scale. This allows for testing, learning, and adjustments while minimizing disruption. For instance, introducing a new software platform to one department first can help identify potential challenges before broader implementation.

5. Provide Clear Communication and Training
   Resistance often stems from fear of the unknown. Leaders should prioritize transparent communication, outlining the reasons for change, its anticipated impact, and the steps involved. Coupling this with comprehensive training ensures team members feel equipped and confident in adopting new practices.

6. Celebrate Wins and Learn from Setbacks
   Highlighting successes, even small ones, can build

momentum and demonstrate the value of change. Conversely, treating setbacks as learning opportunities fosters a culture of continuous improvement and resilience.

Practical Examples of Questioning Norms

Example 1: Transforming Inventory Management
A logistics company relied on manual inventory tracking methods that were prone to errors and delays. The new warehouse manager proposed transitioning to an automated system. By presenting data on error rates and the time spent on manual tasks, engaging employees in selecting and testing the software, and providing robust training, the company achieved a 30% improvement in efficiency within six months.

Example 2: Updating Safety Protocols
In a manufacturing plant, safety procedures had not been revisited in a decade. A leader, noticing an increase in minor incidents, spearheaded a review. By collaborating with employees to identify gaps and implement updated protocols aligned with industry best practices, the plant significantly reduced its incident rate while reinforcing a culture of safety.

Overcoming Resistance to Change

Change often meets resistance, even when well-intentioned. Leaders must address concerns empathetically, recognizing that fear of failure or job displacement can underlie opposition. Strategies for overcoming resistance include:

- Active Listening: Create forums where team members can voice concerns and ask questions, fostering a sense of inclusion and understanding.

- Recognizing Contributions: Highlight how team expertise informed the decision-making process, demonstrating that change isn't imposed but co-created.

- Leading by Example: Show commitment to the new approach by adopting it personally, underscoring its importance and feasibility.

The Ripple Effect of Challenging Norms

When leaders successfully question outdated practices, the benefits extend beyond immediate gains. Teams develop a culture of innovation, where questioning norms becomes not only accepted but encouraged. This proactive mindset can lead to continual improvements, increased adaptability, and a stronger sense of shared purpose.

As industrial leaders embrace their role in challenging the status quo, they unlock untapped potential within their teams and organizations. This subchapter lays the groundwork for fostering a culture where growth and progress thrive.

4.2. Creating an Innovation-Driven Environment

Innovation is the lifeblood of progress in today's fast-evolving industries. For organizations to remain competitive and adaptable, they must prioritize creativity, experimentation, and a willingness to embrace new ideas. Yet, fostering an innovation-driven environment requires more than the occasional brainstorming session—it demands a deliberate cultural shift championed by leaders who inspire, enable, and nurture creative thinking within their teams.

Why Innovation Matters

Industries across the globe are constantly being reshaped by new technologies, consumer demands, and market dynamics. Organizations that fail to innovate risk falling behind, losing relevance, or missing opportunities to excel. Conversely, those that champion innovation often find themselves at the forefront of their fields, leveraging breakthroughs to enhance efficiency, develop new products, and seize market share.

Innovation isn't confined to radical inventions or transformative technologies. It also encompasses incremental improvements that refine processes, enhance customer experiences, and optimize resource utilization. Leaders play a pivotal role in embedding this mindset within their teams, ensuring creativity becomes a core organizational value.

Fostering a Culture of Creativity and Experimentation

Building an innovation-driven environment starts with cultivating a culture that values and rewards creativity. This involves creating an atmosphere where team members feel empowered to share ideas, experiment without fear, and collaborate across boundaries.

1. Encourage Openness and Inclusivity
Innovation thrives in environments where diverse

perspectives come together. Leaders must actively encourage team members to share their ideas, regardless of their role, seniority, or expertise. Inclusivity ensures that no valuable perspective is overlooked, and it fosters a sense of belonging and ownership among all contributors.

2. Lead by Example
Leaders who model creativity and curiosity inspire their teams to do the same. This can include demonstrating a willingness to learn, questioning established practices, and embracing calculated risks. When team members see their leaders taking initiative to innovate, they are more likely to follow suit.

3. Promote Psychological Safety
Team members are unlikely to share bold ideas if they fear criticism, rejection, or repercussions for failure. Leaders must establish an environment of psychological safety, where employees feel respected and supported, regardless of the outcome of their contributions.

Techniques for Driving Innovation

Several practical techniques can help leaders foster creativity and experimentation within their teams:

1. Brainstorming Sessions
Structured brainstorming sessions provide a platform for team members to generate ideas collaboratively. To maximize their effectiveness:

- ➢ Set clear objectives for the session, such as solving a specific problem or exploring new opportunities.

- Use techniques like mind mapping or "blue sky thinking" to encourage out-of-the-box ideas.
- Ensure an open, judgment-free atmosphere where every suggestion is valued.

2. Cross-Functional Collaboration
Innovation often occurs at the intersections of diverse skill sets and knowledge bases. Encouraging cross-functional collaboration enables teams to draw on a wider range of expertise and perspectives. For example, pairing engineers with marketing professionals can yield creative solutions that balance technical feasibility with market appeal.

3. Learning from Failure
Failure is an inevitable part of the innovation process. Instead of penalizing it, leaders should view it as an opportunity to learn and improve. Establishing mechanisms for post-mortem reviews, where teams analyze what went wrong and extract lessons, helps normalize risk-taking and fosters resilience.

4. Resource Allocation for Experimentation
Innovation requires resources, whether it's time, funding, or access to tools and training. Leaders should allocate dedicated resources for experimentation, signaling their commitment to fostering creativity. For instance, setting aside "innovation hours" or establishing small grants for pilot projects can encourage team members to pursue new ideas.

5. Celebrating and Scaling Successes
Recognizing and celebrating successful innovations motivates teams to continue pushing boundaries. Whether it's through awards, public acknowledgment, or tangible

rewards, celebrating creativity reinforces its importance. Leaders should also focus on scaling successful initiatives, ensuring the organization reaps their full benefits.

Practical Examples of Innovation in Action

Example 1: A Retail Chain Embraces Technology
A regional retail chain struggling with inventory management invited employees from multiple departments to brainstorm solutions. The idea of implementing real-time inventory tracking using IoT (Internet of Things) technology emerged from a junior associate in logistics. The company piloted the idea in one location, significantly reducing stockouts and overstocking. With clear success, the system was scaled company-wide, improving customer satisfaction and operational efficiency.

Example 2: A Manufacturing Firm Reduces Waste
A manufacturing firm aiming to reduce production waste initiated a "green innovation challenge," inviting employees to propose eco-friendly solutions. A team of factory workers suggested repurposing scrap materials into packaging for finished products. After testing and refining the process, the initiative reduced waste by 20% and cut packaging costs by 15%.

Challenges and How to Overcome Them

Creating an innovation-driven environment is not without obstacles. Common challenges include resistance to change, resource limitations, and short-term focus. Leaders can address these issues by:

- ➢ Addressing Resistance: Highlight the benefits of innovation, involve skeptics in the process, and ensure changes align with organizational values.
- ➢ Managing Resources: Start small with pilot projects or focus on low-cost solutions before scaling.
- ➢ Balancing Priorities: Emphasize how innovation contributes to long-term success, even when immediate results may not be apparent.

The Ripple Effect of Innovation

When leaders prioritize innovation, they empower their teams to think creatively, take ownership of their ideas, and contribute to the organization's growth. Over time, this mindset becomes self-reinforcing, creating a virtuous cycle where innovation fuels success and inspires further creativity.

By creating an environment that celebrates curiosity and experimentation, leaders pave the way for their teams and organizations to thrive in an ever-changing landscape.

4.3. Strategic Risk-Taking: Balancing Tradition and Progress

Innovation is inherently tied to risk, and while creativity drives progress, poorly managed risks can derail efforts and jeopardize organizational stability. Leaders play a crucial role in navigating this delicate balance, ensuring that new ideas are implemented thoughtfully and align with broader organizational goals. Strategic risk-taking involves evaluating potential gains and pitfalls, fostering innovation while safeguarding against unnecessary disruption.

The Importance of Strategic Risk-Taking

Risk is often perceived negatively, yet it is a necessary component of progress. No breakthrough—whether in technology, processes, or products—occurs without some degree of uncertainty. The key lies in distinguishing between reckless risk and calculated risk. Leaders who can assess risks strategically enable their teams to innovate confidently, fostering an environment where bold ideas are explored responsibly.

Balancing tradition and progress requires a nuanced understanding of the organization's values, goals, and capabilities. Leaders must respect the foundations that have brought the organization success while being open to changes that address evolving needs. Striking this balance ensures continuity while paving the way for growth.

Evaluating Risks in Innovation

Leaders must develop a structured approach to evaluate risks when considering new ideas or changes. This includes:

1. Defining Objectives and Criteria for Success
Before embarking on any initiative, leaders must clearly define the problem they aim to solve and the outcomes they seek to achieve. This clarity provides a benchmark for evaluating whether the proposed solution justifies the associated risks.

2. Assessing Potential Impact and Feasibility
Analyzing the potential impact of a new idea involves

examining both the best-case and worst-case scenarios. Leaders should ask:

> How will this initiative contribute to organizational goals?
> What resources are required, and are they available?
> What are the potential drawbacks, and how can they be mitigated?

3. Engaging Stakeholders
Involving key stakeholders—team members, clients, or partners—in the decision-making process ensures that diverse perspectives inform the evaluation. Stakeholder input can highlight overlooked risks or validate the viability of an idea.

4. Running Pilot Projects
Implementing ideas on a smaller scale allows leaders to test their feasibility and gather data before committing to a full rollout. Pilot projects provide valuable insights into potential challenges, enabling adjustments that reduce risk during broader implementation.

Tools for Risk Assessment

Several tools and frameworks can aid leaders in assessing risks while fostering a culture of creativity:

1. SWOT Analysis (Strengths, Weaknesses, Opportunities, Threats)
This simple yet effective framework helps leaders evaluate internal and external factors that could influence the success of a proposed initiative. By identifying strengths

and opportunities, leaders can build confidence in their decisions, while addressing weaknesses and threats helps mitigate risks.

2. Risk Matrix
A risk matrix plots potential risks based on their likelihood and impact. Categorizing risks as low, medium, or high priority allows leaders to focus on addressing the most significant concerns while proceeding with manageable uncertainties.

3. Scenario Planning
Scenario planning involves envisioning multiple outcomes for a proposed initiative, from best-case to worst-case scenarios. This approach helps leaders anticipate challenges and develop contingency plans, reducing the fear of unknown variables.

4. Cost-Benefit Analysis
Quantifying the potential benefits and costs of an idea provides a clear picture of its value proposition. If the benefits significantly outweigh the risks and costs, the idea may warrant implementation.

Maintaining Creativity While Managing Risks

Risk management should never stifle creativity. Instead, it should serve as a guide that empowers teams to innovate responsibly. Leaders can strike this balance by:

1. Encouraging a Growth Mindset
A growth mindset encourages individuals to view challenges as opportunities to learn rather than as threats. When leaders model this mindset, they create an

environment where calculated risks are embraced as part of the innovation process.

2. Setting Risk Tolerance Levels
Leaders should establish clear parameters for acceptable risk, ensuring teams understand the boundaries within which they can experiment. These parameters provide structure while allowing room for creativity.

3. Emphasizing Resilience and Learning
Not all risks will lead to success, but every experience offers lessons. Leaders should frame setbacks as valuable learning opportunities, reinforcing the idea that failure is a stepping stone to innovation.

Real-World Examples of Strategic Risk-Taking

Example 1: Adopting Automation in Manufacturing
A mid-sized manufacturing company faced rising labor costs and operational inefficiencies. The leadership team decided to pilot automation technologies in one production line. Although the initial investment was significant, the pilot demonstrated improved productivity and reduced errors. With data to support the benefits, the company gradually expanded automation across all operations, achieving substantial cost savings and quality improvements.

Example 2: Expanding into a New Market
A logistics firm identified a growing demand for same-day delivery services in urban areas. Leadership proposed launching a pilot program in one city to test the model. By analyzing customer feedback and operational data, the

company refined its approach before scaling the service nationwide, minimizing financial and reputational risks.

The Leader's Role in Strategic Risk-Taking

Leaders must balance optimism with pragmatism when championing new initiatives. This involves fostering trust within their teams, maintaining transparency about potential risks, and demonstrating a commitment to shared goals. Leaders who navigate risks effectively empower their teams to push boundaries while safeguarding the organization's stability.

Strategic risk-taking is not about avoiding failure entirely but about managing uncertainty in ways that drive progress. By adopting thoughtful evaluation processes, leveraging practical tools, and maintaining a focus on learning and growth, leaders can inspire their teams to innovate confidently and responsibly.

4.4. Leadership in Disruption: Adapting to Change as a Competitive Advantage

In the fast-paced and ever-evolving industrial landscape, the ability to adapt to disruptions is no longer optional but essential for long-term success. Disruptions can emerge from various sources—technological advancements, regulatory shifts, or changing market demands. Effective leaders recognize that managing such changes is not about reacting in the moment but about cultivating a proactive and resilient mindset across their teams. This subchapter explores how leaders can transform disruption from a challenge into a competitive advantage by embracing strategic planning, fostering agility, and leveraging innovation to navigate uncertainty.

Proactive Leadership in Disruption

Disruptive changes often require swift and decisive action, but the groundwork for effective responses begins long before the disruption occurs. Leaders can prepare their teams by maintaining an awareness of industry trends, engaging in continuous learning, and encouraging forward-thinking discussions. For example, a leader who regularly reviews advancements in automation technology can better anticipate its impact on their production processes and workforce requirements. By staying informed, they position their teams to adapt more seamlessly when such technologies become mainstream.

A key aspect of proactive leadership is scenario planning. Leaders should engage their teams in exploring "what-if" scenarios, assessing potential risks and opportunities. For instance, consider a manufacturing plant facing the possibility of supply chain disruptions due to geopolitical factors. Through scenario planning, the leader can identify alternative suppliers, simulate resource allocation strategies, and ensure contingency plans are in place.

Cultivating Resilience Through Agility

Adaptability is at the core of navigating disruption effectively. Leaders must foster an environment where agility is embedded in the team's culture. This involves encouraging a mindset that views change not as a threat but as an opportunity to innovate and improve. One way to achieve this is by implementing agile methodologies in project management. These methodologies prioritize flexibility, iterative progress, and continuous feedback, enabling teams to pivot quickly when faced with unforeseen challenges.

For instance, in the automotive industry, companies transitioning to electric vehicle production faced significant disruptions in supply chains, manufacturing processes, and consumer demand. A leading automaker, recognizing the urgency to innovate, adopted agile principles to accelerate the development of electric vehicles. The company restructured teams to operate in cross-functional units, enabling rapid prototyping and testing of new designs.

This approach allowed them to overcome supply chain bottlenecks by sourcing alternative materials and partners and introduced innovative battery technologies faster than competitors. The leadership's emphasis on experimentation and adaptability empowered the workforce to embrace these challenges, ultimately positioning the company as a market leader in sustainable mobility.

Leveraging Disruption as a Catalyst for Innovation

While disruptions can be challenging, they often present unique opportunities for innovation. Leaders can harness these moments to encourage their teams to think creatively and explore unconventional solutions. This might involve introducing new technologies, reimagining workflows, or developing entirely new products or services to meet emerging needs.

Consider a manufacturing company that adopts smart factory technologies during an industry-wide shift toward automation. By investing in IoT-enabled machinery and predictive maintenance systems, the company not only enhances operational efficiency but also positions itself as a pioneer in its sector. Leaders who champion such initiatives demonstrate that embracing disruption can yield significant competitive advantages.

To foster innovation during disruption, leaders can:

- Encourage brainstorming sessions focused on addressing specific challenges posed by the disruption.
- Create cross-functional teams to combine diverse perspectives and expertise.
- Provide the necessary resources, training, and time for teams to experiment with new ideas.

Tools and Frameworks for Navigating Disruption

Effective leaders rely on structured tools and frameworks to manage disruption strategically. These tools help in assessing the potential impact of changes and devising informed responses. Some key tools include:

- SWOT Analysis: Identifies strengths, weaknesses, opportunities, and threats related to the disruption, offering a clear picture of the organization's position.
- PESTLE Analysis: Examines external factors—political, economic, social, technological, legal, and environmental—that may influence the disruption.

- Technology Audits: Evaluates the readiness and capabilities of current systems to adapt to new technological demands.
- Employee Feedback Mechanisms: Ensures that insights from those directly impacted by the disruption are incorporated into decision-making.

By leveraging these tools, leaders can develop comprehensive strategies that align with both immediate needs and long-term goals.

Building Confidence and Trust During Disruption

Disruptions can create uncertainty and anxiety among team members. Effective leaders prioritize clear communication and transparency to address these concerns. Sharing the rationale behind decisions, outlining the steps being taken to address challenges, and providing regular updates can help build trust and confidence within the team.

Additionally, leaders should acknowledge the emotional impact of disruption and offer support where needed. This might involve providing resources for mental health, offering flexible work arrangements, or simply fostering an open-door policy where team members feel comfortable voicing their concerns.

Lessons Learned: Turning Challenges into Opportunities

Navigating disruption successfully requires not only responding to immediate challenges but also learning from the experience to improve future preparedness. Leaders should take the time to reflect on what worked well and what could be improved, involving their teams in this evaluation process. Documenting these lessons ensures that the organization is better equipped to handle similar situations in the future.

For example, a leader who successfully navigates a shift to remote operations might document the tools, workflows, and communication strategies that enabled the transition. These insights can then inform the organization's approach to hybrid work models or future disruptions.

Conclusion

Leadership during disruption demands a combination of foresight, adaptability, and a commitment to continuous improvement. By preparing proactively, fostering resilience, and leveraging challenges as opportunities for innovation, leaders can turn disruption into a competitive advantage. This subchapter underscores the importance of viewing change not as a hurdle to overcome but as a catalyst for growth and progress, inspiring teams to embrace the future with confidence and determination.

4.5. Case Study 1: Transforming Legacy Processes in Manufacturing – A Leader's Role in Questioning Norms

Background

The XYZ Manufacturing Corporation, a mid-sized company specializing in industrial equipment, had been a key player in its sector for decades. However, the company faced stagnation in its production efficiency and a noticeable decline in market competitiveness. Rooted in traditional practices, XYZ relied on legacy systems and methods that had not been updated for over 20 years. Many employees, including senior managers, were resistant to change, believing that "if it isn't broken, don't fix it."

Challenge

The company's CEO, Avelina Frostwyn, recognized the urgency to modernize operations. Market competitors had embraced automation and data-driven decision-making, leaving XYZ behind. Customers were increasingly favoring rivals with faster production cycles and lower costs. Avelina's challenge was twofold: she had to question the entrenched processes without alienating the team and convince them to adopt a new mindset toward innovation and change.

Strategy

1. Building Trust and Involvement:
   Avelina started by engaging with employees at all levels, listening to their insights and concerns about the existing processes. She made it clear that the goal was not to criticize past practices but to collectively identify areas for improvement. By fostering a sense of shared ownership, Avelina reduced resistance to change and built trust.
2. Data-Driven Advocacy:
   Avelina initiated a thorough assessment of the production process, employing both internal teams and external consultants to identify inefficiencies. The data revealed several pain points: outdated machinery, bottlenecks in assembly lines, and high

operational costs. Sharing these findings transparently with the team created a sense of urgency without assigning blame.
3. Pilot Programs and Gradual Implementation:
Instead of overhauling the entire system at once, Avelina proposed a pilot program to test modern manufacturing techniques, including automation in a single production line. This approach minimized disruption and allowed employees to see the benefits firsthand.
4. Respecting Expertise:
Avelina acknowledged the expertise of long-serving employees, involving them in the redesign process. Their experience was invaluable in identifying practical solutions and ensuring that the new systems were user-friendly.
5. Communication and Training:
Regular workshops, training sessions, and town hall meetings were conducted to address fears and upskill the workforce. Avelina emphasized that modernization was not a threat but an opportunity for growth and skill enhancement.

Outcome

The pilot program's success was undeniable. The automated production line reduced errors by 40%, increased output by 30%, and cut costs significantly. Seeing these tangible benefits, the team was more receptive to scaling the changes across other departments.

Beyond operational improvements, the cultural shift at XYZ was profound. Employees became more open to questioning the status quo and embraced a mindset of continuous improvement. Avelina's respectful approach to challenging norms and fostering collaboration proved instrumental in transforming the organization.

Lessons Learned

- Questioning Norms is Essential for Growth: Entrenched practices can stifle innovation and competitiveness. Leaders must be willing to challenge the status quo to drive progress.
- Respect and Involvement Reduce Resistance: Engaging employees and valuing their expertise fosters trust and cooperation during change initiatives.
- Pilot Programs Build Confidence: Gradual implementation allows teams to adapt to changes without feeling overwhelmed, showcasing the benefits of innovation in manageable steps.
- Data is a Powerful Ally: Presenting objective evidence of inefficiencies can help overcome resistance by framing change as a necessity rather than a choice.

This case demonstrates how a leader's ability to question established practices respectfully can pave the way for innovation, growth, and long-term success. It underscores the importance of balancing tradition with progress, ensuring that organizational evolution is both effective and inclusive.

4.6. Case Study 2: Reinventing a Retail Giant – The Journey of AlphaMartX

Background

AlphaMartX, a well-established retail chain with over 500 stores nationwide, had long been a household name. For decades, its success was built on a tried-and-true model: large physical stores strategically placed in suburban areas, offering a wide range of products at competitive prices. However, the landscape of retail had shifted dramatically with the rise of e-commerce. Tech-savvy competitors like EziCartX and SpeedyShopX had disrupted the industry by providing customers with seamless online shopping experiences and same-day delivery options.

AlphaMartX found itself at a crossroads. While its brand retained strong loyalty among older customers, younger generations were gravitating toward online platforms. Sales had plateaued, and operational costs for maintaining physical stores continued to climb. The management team, led by CEO Nathan Ironvale, faced an uphill battle in transforming AlphaMartX to remain competitive in the digital age.

The Challenge

Nathan understood that AlphaMartX's traditional model was no longer sustainable. However, the company had a deep-rooted culture of adhering to its "golden rules"— principles established decades ago that focused on in-store experiences and avoiding significant risks. Many senior managers resisted the idea of embracing e-commerce, arguing that it would dilute AlphaMartX's identity and alienate its loyal customer base.

Nathan's challenge was multifaceted:

1. Break down the cultural resistance to change and instill a sense of urgency across the organization.
2. Transition from a brick-and-mortar-focused model to an omnichannel strategy without losing the trust of long-time customers.
3. Achieve all of this while maintaining profitability and employee morale.

Strategy

Nathan approached the challenge with a three-pronged strategy: fostering innovation, leveraging data, and building a bridge between tradition and modernity.

1. Fostering a Culture of Innovation
   Nathan understood that to bring about real change, he needed buy-in from employees at all levels. He began by assembling a cross-functional "Innovation Task Force," comprising young, tech-savvy employees and seasoned managers with decades of experience. This diverse group was tasked with identifying pain points in the customer experience and brainstorming solutions.

   To encourage out-of-the-box thinking, Nathan introduced "Innovation Labs" at select stores. These labs served as experimental hubs where employees tested new ideas, from app-based in-store navigation to augmented reality displays for product previews. Employees who contributed successful ideas were publicly recognized and rewarded, fostering a sense of ownership and pride in the transformation journey.

2. Leveraging Data for Insights
Nathan knew that subjective opinions alone would not overcome resistance to change. He commissioned a comprehensive market analysis to understand customer preferences and behaviors. The data revealed that 60% of AlphaMartX's customers preferred online shopping, but they still valued the ability to return items at physical stores.

Armed with these insights, Nathan made a case for an omnichannel approach, where physical and online experiences were seamlessly integrated. His data-driven argument helped sway skeptical managers who had been resistant to moving beyond the traditional model.

3. Balancing Tradition with Modernity
Recognizing the fear of alienating loyal customers, Nathan emphasized that the transformation would enhance—not replace—their in-store experience. He implemented small but impactful changes, such as introducing self-checkout kiosks and loyalty app rewards, which improved efficiency while maintaining a personal touch.

Additionally, AlphaMartX's website was redesigned to mirror the warm and inviting feel of its stores. Features such as video consultations with in-store staff helped retain the human connection that customers valued.

4. Incremental Rollouts and Employee Empowerment
To minimize disruption, Nathan rolled out changes incrementally. Select stores were converted into fulfillment centers for online orders, while others piloted hybrid models offering both in-store and digital services. Employees were trained in digital tools and encouraged to share their feedback on the new systems.

Nathan also held town hall meetings to address employee concerns and highlight success stories. These meetings fostered transparency and trust, ensuring that employees felt like active participants in the transformation rather than passive observers.

Outcome

The results of AlphaMartX's transformation were remarkable. Within three years, online sales accounted for 40% of the company's revenue, up from just 5% before the transformation. In-store traffic stabilized as customers appreciated the hybrid model, which allowed them to shop online and pick up items at their convenience.

AlphaMartX's "Innovation Labs" continued to drive creativity, producing new features such as AI-driven personalized shopping recommendations and real-time inventory updates. Employee morale improved as the company's focus on recognition and empowerment created a more engaged workforce.

The cultural shift was equally significant. Managers who once clung to the "golden rules" became advocates for continuous improvement, realizing that questioning the status quo was essential for survival in a rapidly changing market.

Lessons Learned

- Innovation Requires a Culture Shift: Transforming an organization starts with fostering a mindset of openness and creativity. Recognizing and rewarding employee contributions can drive buy-in and enthusiasm.
- Data-Driven Decision Making is Key: Objective insights help overcome resistance by framing change as a necessity rather than a gamble.
- Balance is Essential: While innovation is critical, respecting core values and traditions ensures that transformation does not alienate loyal stakeholders.
- Incremental Changes Minimize Resistance: Gradual implementation allows teams to adapt and build confidence in new systems, reducing the fear of change.

Broader Implications

AlphaMartX's journey illustrates the importance of leadership in challenging entrenched norms. By questioning "how it's always been done," Nathan Ironvale demonstrated that businesses must evolve to remain relevant. His approach serves as a blueprint for other organizations navigating the delicate balance between honoring tradition and embracing progress.

Chapter 5: Navigating Challenges and Building Resilience

Leadership is often tested not during moments of calm but in times of adversity. Challenges, whether they arise from interpersonal conflicts, skill shortages, or resistance to change, are inevitable in any team or organization. How leaders respond to these challenges determines not only the immediate outcomes but also the long-term health and resilience of the team. A truly effective leader transforms obstacles into opportunities, guiding their team with confidence, empathy, and vision.

At its core, navigating challenges is about understanding and addressing the complexities of human dynamics within the workplace. Conflicts between team members can escalate quickly if not addressed, leading to disengagement, loss of productivity, and a fragmented work environment. Skill gaps, often overlooked, can hinder progress and create frustration, both for those struggling to meet expectations and for those compensating for others. Resistance to change, meanwhile, remains one of the most significant barriers to organizational growth, rooted in fear, uncertainty, and a natural preference for stability. Leaders must recognize these challenges as critical junctures, requiring proactive and thoughtful strategies.

Resilience, both as an individual trait and as a team characteristic, is essential for overcoming these hurdles. Teams that can adapt, recover, and grow stronger in the face of adversity have a competitive edge in today's fast-changing industrial landscape. However, resilience doesn't happen by chance—it must be cultivated. Leaders play a pivotal role in fostering a culture where challenges are viewed as learning opportunities, where effort and growth are valued, and where setbacks are seen as stepping stones rather than insurmountable roadblocks.

This chapter will explore the multifaceted role of leaders in addressing these challenges and building resilience within their teams. It will begin by examining the critical skills and strategies needed to manage interpersonal conflicts, highlighting the importance of empathy, open communication, and mediation. From there, it will delve into identifying and bridging skill gaps, emphasizing the role of mentoring, training, and resource allocation in creating a high-performing team. The third section will address resistance to change, offering actionable techniques for guiding teams through transitions with transparency and trust. The chapter will then focus on cultivating a growth mindset within the team, presenting strategies for encouraging learning, celebrating progress, and fostering innovation. Finally, it will conclude by exploring the concept of resilience as a collective superpower, showcasing how leaders can model and instill this vital trait to prepare their teams for future challenges.

In the following sections, we will provide both theoretical insights and practical tools to help leaders navigate the complexities of modern team management. By the end of this chapter, readers will have a comprehensive understanding of how to confront challenges head-on and build a team that thrives under pressure.

5.1. Managing Interpersonal Conflicts

In every workplace, diverse personalities, priorities, and perspectives intersect daily. While this diversity is an asset that fosters creativity and innovation, it can also lead to interpersonal conflicts if not carefully managed. These conflicts, if unresolved, can escalate and negatively impact team morale, productivity, and overall workplace harmony. For leaders, the ability to mediate disputes, encourage dialogue, and restore balance is a critical skill that underscores their effectiveness in guiding teams.

Understanding the Root Causes of Workplace Conflicts

Interpersonal conflicts rarely arise in isolation. They are often the product of deeper underlying issues, including:

1. Misunderstandings: Communication breakdowns are among the most common causes of conflict. Misinterpretation of emails, unclear verbal instructions, or lack of context can lead to friction. For example, a team member may perceive a colleague's direct feedback as overly critical, creating tension.
2. Competing Priorities: Departments or individuals with different objectives may find themselves at odds when resources, deadlines, or goals clash. For instance, a production team might feel pressure to meet output targets, while the quality assurance team emphasizes thorough inspections, creating a natural but manageable conflict.
3. Differing Work Styles: Variations in personality, decision-making approaches, and work habits can lead to misunderstandings. A highly detail-oriented

employee might struggle to collaborate with a colleague who prioritizes speed and efficiency over precision, leading to frustration on both sides.
4. Perceived Inequity: A sense of unfairness in workload distribution, recognition, or access to opportunities often breeds resentment. If left unaddressed, these feelings can fester and create divisions within the team.

The Leader's Role in Conflict Resolution

Leaders are not just observers in situations of conflict; they must actively facilitate resolutions that uphold team cohesion and trust. The following tools and approaches can empower leaders to manage conflicts effectively:

1. Active Listening
The cornerstone of conflict resolution is ensuring that all parties feel heard. Leaders must approach disputes with neutrality and focus on understanding each individual's perspective. Active listening involves maintaining eye contact, asking clarifying questions, and repeating back key points to confirm understanding. For example, if two employees disagree about project priorities, a leader might say, "What I'm hearing is that you feel your deadlines are being overlooked, while your colleague is concerned about resource constraints. Is that accurate?"

2. Encouraging Open Communication
Creating a safe environment where team members can express their concerns without fear of judgment is essential. Leaders should establish ground rules for respectful dialogue, such as avoiding blame and focusing

on solutions. Mediated conversations often help identify shared goals and areas of compromise.

3. Identifying Common Ground

Even in the most heated disputes, there are usually shared objectives that can serve as a foundation for resolution. Leaders can steer the conversation toward these points, emphasizing the team's overarching mission and mutual interests. For example, in a disagreement between a sales team and a logistics team, the shared goal of delivering exceptional customer service can be a unifying focus.

4. Adopting a Problem-Solving Approach

Shifting the focus from assigning blame to collaboratively solving the problem is critical. Leaders should guide the discussion toward actionable solutions rather than dwelling on past grievances. For example, if workload imbalances are causing tension, a leader might suggest redistributing tasks or implementing a transparent scheduling system to ensure fairness.

Proactive Strategies to Prevent Conflict

While resolving existing conflicts is vital, proactive measures can minimize their occurrence:

- Fostering a Culture of Respect: Leaders should model and promote respect in all interactions. Recognizing and celebrating diversity, setting clear behavioral expectations, and addressing inappropriate conduct promptly can create a foundation of mutual respect.
- Team Building Activities: Regular team-building exercises can enhance understanding and

camaraderie among team members, reducing the likelihood of conflicts stemming from misunderstandings or unfamiliarity.
- ➢ Clear Role Definitions: Ambiguity in roles and responsibilities often leads to disputes. By clearly outlining expectations and accountability, leaders can prevent confusion and overlap.
- ➢ Conflict Management Training: Providing team members with tools to navigate conflicts independently, such as workshops on communication styles or negotiation techniques, empowers them to handle disagreements constructively.

When to Escalate Conflicts

While most conflicts can be resolved within the team, some require escalation. Situations involving harassment, discrimination, or repeated violations of workplace policies should be handled with the involvement of human resources or higher management. Leaders must ensure that these issues are addressed promptly and appropriately to maintain a safe and equitable work environment.

A Balanced Approach to Leadership in Conflict

Managing interpersonal conflicts is not about suppressing differences but about leveraging them to create a stronger, more cohesive team. Leaders who approach conflicts with empathy, transparency, and a problem-solving mindset demonstrate their commitment to fostering a positive work environment. Moreover, when teams see their leader successfully navigating challenges, they gain confidence in their ability to collaborate and overcome future disputes.

By addressing interpersonal conflicts effectively, leaders pave the way for enhanced trust, communication, and collaboration within their teams. These foundations are crucial for achieving long-term success and resilience in any organization.

5.2. Bridging Skill Gaps for a High-Performing Team

Skill gaps within a team are inevitable in today's dynamic work environment, where industries evolve rapidly, and roles often require expertise across a wide spectrum of disciplines. Leaders must approach these gaps proactively, viewing them not as liabilities but as opportunities for growth. To bridge skill gaps effectively, it's essential to adopt a multifaceted strategy that combines targeted training, collaborative mentoring, and leveraging team strengths. Additionally, integrating skill development into daily workflows ensures that learning is not perceived as an added burden but as a seamless part of organizational culture.

One of the most effective ways to address skill gaps is through structured mentoring programs. Pairing less experienced team members with seasoned professionals fosters knowledge transfer, creates opportunities for hands-on learning, and strengthens team cohesion. For example, a marketing team struggling with analytics may benefit from senior analysts mentoring junior members to build competency in data interpretation and campaign optimization. Such initiatives not only fill immediate skill shortages but also nurture a culture of shared learning.

Formal training programs are equally vital, especially when new tools or methodologies are introduced. However, training alone is often insufficient. To ensure the retention and practical application of skills, leaders must embed learning into everyday tasks. This could involve assigning projects that challenge employees to apply their new knowledge, providing feedback loops for continuous improvement, and encouraging team members to share insights gained from external courses or workshops.

The Role of Coaching in Bridging Skill Gaps

While mentoring and training are invaluable, coaching offers a personalized and dynamic approach to development that addresses individual strengths and challenges. Unlike mentoring, which often focuses on long-term career growth, coaching is action-oriented and targeted at immediate performance improvement. Leaders who adopt a coaching mindset work closely with team members to set specific goals, identify obstacles, and develop tailored solutions.

For example, imagine a project manager struggling to prioritize tasks effectively. A leader acting as a coach might observe their workflow, provide constructive feedback, and work collaboratively to develop better time-management strategies. Similarly, coaching can be used to address softer skills, such as improving communication in client-facing roles or building confidence during presentations.

The benefits of coaching extend beyond skill development. It fosters trust and motivation, strengthens the leader-employee relationship, and creates an environment where team members feel supported in their professional growth. To implement coaching effectively, leaders should adopt techniques such as one-on-one sessions, role-playing scenarios, and real-time feedback during projects.

Leveraging Team Strengths to Offset Skill Gaps

Another key strategy is recognizing and leveraging individual strengths within the team to compensate for weaknesses. This requires leaders to have a deep understanding of their team members' capabilities and work styles. For instance, if one team member excels in technical problem-solving but lacks communication skills, pairing them with a colleague who is a natural communicator can create a balanced dynamic that benefits the entire project.

Continuous Feedback and Upskilling

Skill development is not a one-time endeavor but an ongoing process. Leaders should establish mechanisms for continuous feedback, enabling employees to identify areas of improvement and measure their progress. Upskilling can also be integrated into routine workflows, such as assigning stretch projects or rotating roles within the team to expose employees to new challenges.

By combining mentoring, training, coaching, and leveraging team strengths, leaders can effectively bridge skill gaps and create a high-performing team. These approaches ensure that employees are not only equipped to meet current demands but are also prepared for future challenges.

5.3. Overcoming Resistance to Change

Change is an inevitable aspect of organizational growth and innovation, yet it often meets resistance from employees and even leaders themselves. This resistance is not merely a matter of stubbornness; it is deeply rooted in emotional and psychological factors, including fear of the unknown, loss of control, and uncertainty about personal or professional impact. For leaders, understanding the underlying reasons for resistance and addressing them with empathy and strategy is essential for ensuring successful transitions.

This subchapter explores the multifaceted nature of resistance to change, delving into its causes and providing actionable techniques for leaders to foster trust, build transparency, and guide their teams through challenging transitions.

The Psychology of Resistance

Resistance to change often stems from fear—fear of failure, job loss, or inadequacy in adapting to new systems or expectations. Employees may worry that their current skills will become obsolete or that they will lose the comfort of familiarity. Additionally, individuals may resist change due to cognitive biases, such as the "status quo bias," which causes people to favor existing conditions over potential risks, even if the latter promises significant benefits.

From a psychological perspective, change disrupts routines and challenges individuals to rewire established behaviors. This can trigger stress, frustration, and even disengagement if not managed effectively. Leaders must recognize that resistance is often a natural and human response to change, rather than a direct challenge to authority or progress.

The Role of Trust in Navigating Change

Trust is the cornerstone of overcoming resistance to change. Employees are more likely to embrace transitions when they believe their leaders are acting transparently and in their best interests. A lack of trust, on the other hand, exacerbates resistance, leading to skepticism about motives, plans, and outcomes.

To build trust, leaders should prioritize open and honest communication. Sharing the reasons behind proposed changes, the expected benefits, and the potential challenges demonstrates transparency and aligns the team with the organization's goals. For example, if a company plans to implement a new software platform, leaders can explain how it will streamline workflows, reduce redundancies, and free up time for more strategic tasks. Inviting questions and addressing concerns openly helps to alleviate fears and build confidence in the decision.

Techniques to Address Resistance

1. Empathy and Active Listening
   Leaders must empathize with employees' concerns and actively listen to their feedback. This involves creating a safe space for individuals to voice their fears or frustrations without fear of reprisal. For instance, holding regular team discussions or anonymous surveys can provide valuable insights

into the sources of resistance. Leaders who validate these emotions and demonstrate understanding build stronger rapport and trust within their teams.
2. Involving Employees in the Change Process
Resistance often diminishes when employees feel a sense of ownership in the change process. Leaders can achieve this by involving team members in decision-making, seeking their input on implementation strategies, and empowering them to lead smaller aspects of the transition. For example, appointing change champions—employees who advocate for and support the transition—can help create a ripple effect of positivity and cooperation.
3. Tailored Communication Strategies
A one-size-fits-all communication approach rarely works in times of change. Leaders should tailor their messages to different groups within the organization, addressing specific concerns and emphasizing the aspects of change that resonate most with each audience. For example, a technical team may require detailed explanations of how new tools will improve efficiency, while a sales team may focus on how the change will enhance customer interactions.
4. Gradual Implementation
Introducing change incrementally can mitigate resistance by giving employees time to adapt and adjust. For instance, rather than implementing a company-wide software overhaul overnight, leaders can roll out the change department by department, providing training and support along the way. This phased approach allows for early

identification of challenges and provides opportunities for feedback and adjustment.
5. Recognizing and Rewarding Adaptability
Positive reinforcement is a powerful motivator. Recognizing and rewarding employees who embrace change demonstrates that adaptability is valued and appreciated. This can be as simple as public acknowledgment in team meetings or more formal rewards, such as professional development opportunities for those who lead by example during transitions.

Overcoming Deep-Seated Resistance

In some cases, resistance to change persists despite a leader's best efforts. When this happens, it's essential to address the root causes at an individual level. One-on-one coaching sessions can help uncover personal concerns or barriers, while offering tailored solutions to ease the transition. For example, if an employee fears they lack the skills needed for a new role, providing targeted training or mentorship can alleviate their anxiety.

When resistance stems from cultural or systemic issues, leaders may need to take a broader approach, reevaluating organizational values, processes, or incentives that inadvertently reinforce the status quo. For example, if an organization's performance metrics reward adherence to established processes rather than innovation, employees may perceive change as a threat to their job security.

The Long-Term Impact of Change Management

Successfully navigating resistance to change has long-term benefits that extend beyond the immediate transition. Teams that overcome initial resistance and adapt to new ways of working often emerge stronger, more cohesive, and more resilient. These experiences build a foundation of trust and flexibility that prepares the organization for future challenges.

Focusing on empathy, transparency, and engagement, leaders can transform resistance to change into an opportunity for growth and innovation. As organizations face an ever-accelerating pace of change in the modern workplace, mastering the art of change management becomes a vital skill for any leader.

5.4. Cultivating a Growth Mindset in the Team

In the ever-evolving landscape of modern industries, the ability to learn, adapt, and grow is no longer optional—it is a prerequisite for success. A growth mindset, a term popularized by psychologist Carol Dweck, refers to the belief that abilities and intelligence can be developed through dedication, effort, and learning. For leaders, instilling this mindset within their teams is a powerful strategy for fostering innovation, resilience, and long-term success.

This subchapter explores the concept of a growth mindset in depth, emphasizing its significance in team culture and dynamics. It also provides actionable strategies for leaders to nurture this mindset, rewarding effort, encouraging continuous learning, and celebrating incremental progress.

The Importance of a Growth Mindset

A growth mindset contrasts with a fixed mindset, where individuals believe their talents and intelligence are static traits. In a team with a fixed mindset, fear of failure, resistance to feedback, and aversion to challenges can stifle progress. Conversely, a team that embraces a growth mindset views challenges as opportunities, feedback as constructive, and setbacks as steps in the learning process.

For example, in an organization navigating digital transformation, employees with a growth mindset are more likely to embrace new technologies, learn new skills, and contribute to innovative solutions. This mindset creates a culture of adaptability and proactive problem-solving, empowering the team to thrive in uncertain environments.

Strategies for Cultivating a Growth Mindset

1. Model the Growth Mindset as a Leader
   Leadership sets the tone for team culture. Leaders who openly demonstrate a growth mindset—by seeking feedback, acknowledging their own areas for improvement, and embracing challenges—encourage their teams to do the same. For instance, a manager who shares their learning process after attending a professional development workshop signals that growth is a continuous journey, not a destination.
2. Create a Safe Space for Learning and Experimentation
   Fear of failure is a major barrier to adopting a growth mindset. Leaders can counter this by

fostering an environment where experimentation and learning are valued over perfection. For example, implementing a "fail fast, learn faster" policy encourages team members to try new approaches without fear of judgment. Regular debriefs after projects—both successful and unsuccessful—can focus on extracting lessons rather than assigning blame.

3. Reward Effort and Persistence, Not Just Outcomes
   Traditional reward systems often focus solely on results, inadvertently discouraging risk-taking and experimentation. To cultivate a growth mindset, leaders should recognize and reward effort, perseverance, and creativity. For example, celebrating an employee who proposed an innovative solution, even if it didn't yield immediate results, reinforces the value of initiative and learning.

4. Encourage Constructive Feedback
   Feedback is a cornerstone of growth, but its delivery and reception are equally important. Leaders should train their teams to provide constructive feedback that focuses on improvement rather than criticism. Similarly, leaders must model receptiveness to feedback, demonstrating that even those in senior positions can learn and grow.

5. Embed Learning into Daily Workflows
   Opportunities for learning should not be limited to formal training sessions. Leaders can integrate learning into everyday tasks by encouraging cross-functional collaboration, knowledge-sharing sessions, or even dedicating time during team meetings to discuss new insights or industry trends.

For example, a "weekly learning spotlight" where team members share a valuable resource or lesson can inspire ongoing curiosity and growth.
6. Celebrate Small Wins
Progress often happens incrementally, and recognizing these small milestones builds momentum and motivation. For instance, if a team successfully implements a new process after a series of iterations, acknowledging this achievement reinforces the value of persistence and improvement. Celebrations don't have to be elaborate; even a simple acknowledgment during a meeting can boost morale and encourage continued effort.

The Role of Challenges in Growth

Challenges and obstacles are opportunities to cultivate a growth mindset. Leaders should frame these experiences as learning moments rather than setbacks. For example, if a project faces unexpected delays due to external factors, the team can analyze what adjustments were made and how similar scenarios can be handled more effectively in the future. This approach transforms challenges into stepping stones for development.

Moreover, leaders can introduce "stretch assignments" to push team members slightly outside their comfort zones. By gradually increasing responsibilities and supporting employees through these challenges, leaders can foster both confidence and competence within their teams.

Cultivating a Long-Term Growth Culture

While individual initiatives can spark a growth mindset, sustaining it requires embedding the principles into the organization's culture. Leaders can work to align performance metrics, reward systems, and organizational values with growth-oriented behaviors. For example, prioritizing innovation and learning as key performance indicators reinforces the importance of continuous improvement.

Additionally, hiring practices can emphasize candidates who demonstrate curiosity, adaptability, and a willingness to learn. By building teams that inherently value growth, leaders create a foundation for ongoing success.

Measuring the Impact of a Growth Mindset

The effectiveness of a growth mindset can be gauged through both qualitative and quantitative measures. Leaders might observe an increase in employee engagement, collaboration, and willingness to tackle new challenges. On a broader scale, improved innovation rates, faster adaptation to changes, and enhanced team resilience serve as tangible indicators of success.

The Connection to Leadership Excellence

Fostering a growth mindset within a team is a reflection of effective leadership. It not only empowers employees to achieve their full potential but also positions the organization for sustained growth and innovation. As leaders continue to cultivate this mindset, they pave the way for a more adaptive, innovative, and resilient workforce.

5.5. Resilience as a Team Superpower

In the face of evolving market dynamics, rapid technological advancements, and unforeseen crises, resilience stands out as one of the most critical attributes a team can possess. Resilience is more than just the ability to bounce back from setbacks; it is the capacity to adapt, learn, and thrive despite challenges. For leaders, cultivating resilience within their teams not only ensures stability during difficult times but also creates a foundation for sustained success and innovation.

This subchapter delves into the concept of resilience as a collective strength, emphasizing the leader's role in fostering a resilient team culture. It explores practical strategies, from proactive planning and adaptability to providing emotional support, and highlights how resilience transforms adversity into opportunity.

The Significance of Team Resilience

At its core, resilience reflects a team's ability to navigate through uncertainty while maintaining focus, motivation, and collaboration. In high-pressure industries, where setbacks such as project delays, budget constraints, or shifting priorities are common, resilience becomes a superpower that separates high-performing teams from those that falter.

For instance, consider a product development team facing a major setback due to a regulatory change. A resilient team, rather than succumbing to frustration, views the challenge as an opportunity to innovate. By leveraging their collective strengths and maintaining a positive outlook, they adapt their approach to meet new requirements while remaining committed to their goals.

Modeling Resilience as a Leader

Leadership sets the tone for resilience within a team. Leaders who demonstrate composure, adaptability, and determination in the face of adversity inspire their teams to follow suit. Some ways leaders can model resilience include:

- Embracing Change: Leaders who approach change with an open mind and a solutions-oriented attitude set an example for their teams. For instance, a manager who actively seeks creative solutions during a budget cut signals that obstacles are temporary and solvable.
- Sharing Personal Stories: By openly discussing their own challenges and how they overcame them, leaders humanize the resilience-building process, showing that setbacks are part of growth.
- Focusing on What Can Be Controlled: Resilient leaders help their teams concentrate on actionable steps rather than dwelling on uncontrollable factors, fostering a sense of empowerment.

Building a Resilient Team Culture

1. **Encouraging Proactive Planning**
   Resilience begins with preparation. Leaders can guide their teams in identifying potential risks and

developing contingency plans. For example, a marketing team launching a new product might create alternative campaigns to address unexpected market reactions, ensuring they remain agile and responsive.

2. **Promoting Adaptability**
   The ability to pivot quickly in response to change is a hallmark of resilience. Leaders can foster adaptability by encouraging experimentation and flexibility in workflows. Cross-functional projects, where team members step into unfamiliar roles, help build a versatile and agile team.

3. **Developing Strong Communication Channels**
   Transparent and open communication is essential during challenging times. Leaders should create an environment where team members feel comfortable sharing concerns, seeking support, and offering solutions. Regular check-ins and clear updates help reduce uncertainty and maintain trust.

4. **Focusing on Strengths**
   Resilient teams leverage their individual and collective strengths to overcome obstacles. Leaders can conduct strength assessments and assign roles that align with team members' capabilities, ensuring that everyone contributes effectively during critical periods.

5. **Celebrating Milestones, Big and Small**
   Recognizing achievements, no matter how minor, reinforces a team's sense of accomplishment and motivates them to keep pushing forward. For example, if a sales team achieves a milestone despite economic downturns, celebrating their

effort acknowledges their resilience and builds morale.

Providing Emotional Support and Well-Being

Resilience is not purely strategic; it also involves emotional strength. Leaders who prioritize their team's well-being create a supportive atmosphere that enhances collective resilience. Key strategies include:

- Active Listening: Providing a space for team members to express their frustrations or concerns helps alleviate stress and fosters a sense of solidarity.
- Well-Being Initiatives: Offering mental health resources, stress management workshops, or even informal wellness activities can reduce burnout and enhance resilience.
- Empathy and Understanding: Leaders who show genuine care for their team members' challenges cultivate trust and loyalty, key components of a resilient culture.

Learning and Growing from Setbacks

Resilience isn't just about recovery; it's about growth. Leaders can encourage their teams to reflect on setbacks and identify valuable lessons. For example, after a project delay caused by resource shortages, a team might analyze what processes could be improved to prevent similar issues in the future. This approach transforms challenges into opportunities for continuous improvement.

Additionally, creating a culture where mistakes are viewed as learning opportunities rather than failures reduces the fear of taking risks, fostering a mindset of innovation and resilience.

The Long-Term Benefits of Resilience

Teams that prioritize resilience are better equipped to handle both short-term disruptions and long-term challenges. They adapt more effectively to industry changes, maintain higher levels of engagement and motivation, and contribute to a culture of continuous growth. Resilient teams are also more likely to innovate, as they view obstacles as opportunities to explore new approaches and solutions.

Conclusion: A Collective Superpower

Resilience is not an innate trait but a skill that can be nurtured and developed through intentional leadership. By modeling resilience, fostering a supportive culture, and empowering teams to embrace challenges, leaders transform adversity into a collective superpower that drives success.

5.6. Case Study 1: Transforming a Team through Skill Development and Conflict Resolution

In a mid-sized manufacturing company, the engineering department was struggling to meet project deadlines. The team faced mounting pressure from leadership due to frequent errors and inefficiencies. The department head, Martina Stormriven, had recently taken over the role and quickly identified two critical issues: a noticeable skill gap among team members and ongoing interpersonal conflicts.

The skill gap stemmed from the team's transition to using advanced automation technology. While some employees excelled with the new tools, others struggled to adapt. Simultaneously, conflicts between senior and junior staff created a tense environment. Senior employees resisted change, blaming the juniors for errors, while the younger staff felt unsupported and undervalued.

Step 1: Diagnosing the Problems

Martina began by conducting one-on-one interviews with each team member. She asked open-ended questions about their challenges, perceptions of the work environment, and aspirations for personal development. This process revealed:

- Senior staff felt threatened by the juniors' familiarity with the new technology and feared their roles might become redundant.
- Junior staff wanted mentorship but felt dismissed when asking for guidance.
- Both groups lacked sufficient training in the new automation processes.

Step 2: Bridging Skill Gaps with Customized Training

Martina implemented a multi-phase training program tailored to the team's needs:

1. Foundational Workshops: These sessions provided hands-on training for all employees, ensuring

everyone had a baseline understanding of the new tools.
2. Peer Learning: Martina paired senior and junior employees in mentorship-style partnerships. This allowed juniors to learn from the seniors' experience while helping the seniors build confidence with the new technology.
3. Ongoing Development: She introduced a budget for continuous professional development, allowing employees to attend external workshops or obtain certifications.

Step 3: Resolving Conflicts and Rebuilding Trust

Recognizing the need for a culture shift, Martina facilitated open discussions to address underlying tensions. In these sessions:

- ➢ Team members shared their frustrations and aspirations in a safe, moderated environment.
- ➢ Martina emphasized the value of diverse skill sets, showing how juniors' tech-savviness and seniors' institutional knowledge were complementary.
- ➢ Ground rules for communication were established, prioritizing respect and collaboration.

Step 4: Measuring and Celebrating Success

As the training progressed, Martina tracked performance metrics such as project completion rates, error reduction, and team satisfaction scores. Within six months:

- ➢ Errors decreased by 40%, and deadlines were consistently met.

- Cross-generational collaboration flourished, with team members reporting improved relationships.
- Employee retention increased as both junior and senior staff felt more valued.

Conclusion

Martina's approach highlights the power of addressing skill gaps and interpersonal conflicts simultaneously. By fostering open communication, promoting mentorship, and prioritizing professional growth, she transformed a dysfunctional team into a high-performing unit.

5.7. Case Study 2: Building Team Resilience to Navigate an Industry Shift

At EvergreenXYZ Solutions, a mid-sized environmental consulting firm, external pressures were mounting. Regulatory changes in sustainable practices and the rise of artificial intelligence (AI)-powered tools were reshaping the industry. The firm's traditional approach to environmental assessment, which relied on manual data collection and analysis, was no longer competitive.

The company's leadership tasked Felix Feylock, the newly appointed operations manager, with steering the team through this transformation. Felix faced two immediate challenges:

1. Adapting to technological disruptions: The team had minimal experience with AI tools and feared they would lose relevance in their roles.

2. Maintaining morale during change: Employees were skeptical about the shift, doubting its necessity and fearing job loss.

Step 1: Creating a Vision for Change

Felix began by holding a town hall meeting to outline the reasons for embracing AI-powered tools and how they aligned with the company's mission of providing innovative, sustainable solutions. He highlighted:

- The increasing demand for faster and more accurate environmental assessments.
- The opportunity to reduce manual workload and focus on strategic problem-solving.

Felix stressed that technology would enhance, not replace, employees' roles. He framed the change as a shared opportunity for growth.

Step 2: Equipping the Team with Skills

Recognizing the team's resistance stemmed from a lack of familiarity with AI, Felix rolled out a structured learning and development program:

- Training Bootcamps: He partnered with a local tech institute to offer customized AI workshops, giving employees hands-on experience.
- In-House Pilots: Small groups experimented with AI tools on less critical projects, gaining confidence without the pressure of high stakes.

- Mentorship Programs: Felix assigned tech-savvy employees as mentors to help their peers navigate the new tools.

Step 3: Encouraging Resilience Through Small Wins

To build resilience, Felix broke the transformation into manageable phases, celebrating each success:

- After the first pilot project, the team reduced analysis time by 30%. Felix showcased this achievement in a company-wide presentation, crediting the team for their adaptability.
- Employees who completed training certifications received recognition at monthly meetings.

By tying milestones to tangible results, Felix reinforced the value of embracing change.

Step 4: Addressing Emotional Resistance

Felix didn't overlook the emotional toll of change. He implemented:

- Anonymous Feedback Channels: Employees could voice concerns without fear of judgment.
- Regular Check-Ins: Felix held one-on-one meetings to address individual anxieties and offer support.
- Stress-Management Workshops: Partnering with HR, he organized sessions on coping with change and fostering mental well-being.

Step 5: Embedding a Resilient Culture

To sustain momentum, Felix embedded resilience into the company's culture:

- He introduced quarterly innovation days, where employees could pitch and experiment with new ideas.
- Teams were encouraged to document lessons from failures, normalizing setbacks as learning opportunities.
- Felix adopted a "leader-as-coach" approach, guiding the team to independently solve problems and embrace challenges.

Outcome

Within a year, EvergreenXYZ Solutions became a leader in AI-powered environmental consulting, landing three high-profile contracts with major clients. Employee engagement scores improved by 35%, and the company reduced staff turnover by half. The team no longer viewed technological disruptions as threats but as opportunities for growth.

Conclusion

Felix's leadership demonstrated that resilience isn't just about weathering storms—it's about thriving in their aftermath. By addressing both technical and emotional needs, he turned a resistant team into a forward-thinking, adaptable workforce ready to tackle the challenges of a rapidly changing industry.

Part 3: Leading by Example

"Leadership isn't a role to play, it's a responsibility to show others the way."

Chapter 6: Leading with Authenticity and Purpose

In an era defined by rapid change and constant disruption, leadership rooted in authenticity has emerged as a beacon of stability and inspiration. Authentic leaders are those who lead with integrity, aligning their actions with their core values and beliefs. They inspire trust, foster collaboration, and create a sense of belonging within their teams. This chapter explores the transformative power of authenticity in leadership, emphasizing how it serves as the cornerstone of meaningful and effective leadership.

Authenticity in leadership is not about projecting a perfect image; rather, it is about embracing one's true self, complete with strengths, weaknesses, and imperfections. Leaders who are authentic demonstrate a willingness to listen, learn, and adapt, cultivating an environment where their team members feel safe to do the same. This openness breaks down hierarchical barriers, creating a dynamic where creativity, innovation, and honest communication can flourish. By prioritizing authenticity, leaders can build a foundation of trust that strengthens team cohesion and resilience in the face of challenges.

Purpose is the driving force behind authentic leadership. When leaders lead with purpose, they provide their teams with a clear sense of direction and meaning. Purpose fuels motivation, fosters alignment, and transforms routine tasks into fulfilling contributions toward a larger goal. In today's workplace, where employees seek more than just a paycheck, leaders who connect daily work to a broader mission can elevate team morale, productivity, and loyalty.

This chapter provides a comprehensive exploration of what it means to lead with authenticity and purpose. It delves into the traits and behaviors that define authentic leaders, including humility, transparency, and consistency. It also examines how leaders can cultivate a culture of purpose within their organizations, ensuring that every team member feels valued and connected to the organization's overarching mission.

Furthermore, the chapter highlights the ripple effect of authenticity, showcasing how leaders who "walk the talk" influence not just their immediate teams but the broader organizational culture. By living out their values, leaders set an example that inspires others to follow suit, creating a legacy of trust, integrity, and shared vision.

The journey to authentic leadership is not a destination but an ongoing process of self-discovery, growth, and alignment. Through actionable insights, practical tools, and real-world examples, this chapter equips leaders to embrace their true selves and lead with confidence, purpose, and impact.

6.1. Walking the Talk: Actions Speak Louder Than Words

Leadership is defined not just by words but by actions. The principle that "actions speak louder than words" is especially relevant in leadership, as a leader's behavior sets the tone for the entire team. When actions align with words, they communicate values and expectations clearly, fostering trust and inspiring the team to perform at their best.

Walking the talk involves embodying the principles and values that leaders expect their teams to follow. A lack of alignment between what a leader says and does can create confusion and erode trust. Conversely, leaders who demonstrate integrity, honor their commitments, and consistently model the behaviors they wish to see in others establish a solid foundation for a productive and unified team culture. By leading through consistent actions, leaders build credibility and inspire their teams to adopt shared values and work towards common goals.

6.1.1. Authenticity as the Foundation of Leadership

Authenticity is at the core of effective leadership. It is the ability to be genuine, transparent, and true to oneself while respecting and valuing the individuality of others. Authentic leaders do not put on a façade to impress or manipulate others; instead, they lead from a place of honesty and integrity. This quality is vital for establishing trust, which is the foundation of strong relationships and high-performing teams.

Why Authenticity Matters in Leadership

Authenticity fosters a sense of connection. When leaders are authentic, they create an environment where team members feel comfortable being themselves. This openness encourages honest communication, builds mutual respect, and strengthens team cohesion. A leader who is authentic shows that they are human, which makes them relatable and approachable, encouraging their team to share ideas, concerns, and feedback freely.

Moreover, authenticity builds credibility. Teams are more likely to trust and follow a leader who consistently acts in alignment with their values and promises. When words match actions, it signals integrity, which is crucial for long-term influence. For example, if a leader emphasizes the importance of collaboration but frequently takes credit for the team's achievements without acknowledgment, their credibility erodes. Conversely, an authentic leader who attributes success to their team and gives credit where it is due earns respect and loyalty.

Challenges to Authentic Leadership

Despite its importance, being an authentic leader is not without challenges. Leaders often face pressures to conform to expectations, fit into predefined molds, or avoid vulnerability to appear more authoritative. However, these pressures can lead to inconsistency between a leader's actions and their true values, diminishing their authenticity.

Leaders may also struggle with balancing transparency and discretion. While authenticity demands honesty, leaders must carefully consider how much information to share to maintain professionalism and protect sensitive matters. Navigating this balance requires wisdom and emotional intelligence.

Another challenge arises when leaders fear being judged or misunderstood. Authenticity does not guarantee universal approval; in fact, it may provoke resistance from those uncomfortable with change or differing perspectives. However, the long-term benefits of authentic leadership—trust, respect, and loyalty—far outweigh the short-term discomfort it may cause.

How to Cultivate Authenticity as a Leader

1. Know Your Values: Start by identifying your core principles and what truly matters to you. Understanding your values allows you to make decisions and take actions that align with them, creating consistency in your leadership.
2. Practice Self-Awareness: Reflect on your strengths, weaknesses, and areas for growth. Authentic leaders are not afraid to acknowledge their imperfections and seek opportunities to improve. Regular self-assessment helps ensure your actions align with your intentions.
3. Be Transparent: Share your thought processes, goals, and challenges with your team. Transparency fosters trust and shows that you value their input. For example, if a project faces delays, explain the reasons openly and involve the team in finding solutions.
4. Show Vulnerability: Authentic leaders are willing to admit when they make mistakes or don't have all the answers. Vulnerability demonstrates humility and creates a safe space for team members to be honest about their own challenges.
5. Stay Consistent: Ensure your actions align with your words, even in challenging situations. For instance, if you prioritize work-life balance, model it by respecting your own boundaries and encouraging your team to do the same.
6. Adapt Without Compromising Core Values: Authenticity does not mean being rigid. Effective

leaders adapt to changing circumstances while staying true to their principles. Flexibility in approach paired with consistency in values ensures authenticity in action.

Authentic Leadership in Action

An excellent example of authentic leadership is a manager who leads by example during challenging times. Imagine a leader advocating for teamwork and collaboration. Instead of merely encouraging others, they actively participate in problem-solving sessions, take responsibility for failures, and openly celebrate the team's collective achievements. This behavior not only reinforces their commitment to teamwork but also inspires others to emulate their approach.

Authenticity can also shine in small but impactful gestures. For instance, a leader who personally checks in with team members during stressful periods, listens empathetically, and provides genuine encouragement demonstrates their commitment to the team's well-being. These actions build trust and reinforce the leader's authenticity.

By embracing authenticity, leaders can foster trust, loyalty, and a culture of mutual respect. This creates a strong foundation for their teams to thrive and ensures that leadership influence is both meaningful and enduring.

6.1.2. The Impact of Consistent Actions

Consistency in leadership is not merely about fulfilling promises; it is about reinforcing the standards and values that a leader wants their team to embody. By aligning behavior with expectations, leaders create a powerful ripple effect, where their actions shape the culture, norms, and performance of the team.

Behavioral Foundations of Leadership

The behavioral aspect of "walking the talk" lies in the alignment between what a leader says and how they act. When leaders consistently model the behaviors they expect from their teams—be it accountability, innovation, or collaboration—they establish an unspoken agreement. Team members observe these actions and often mirror them, naturally embedding the desired practices into their workflows. For example, a leader who prioritizes continuous learning by attending training sessions or engaging with industry trends inspires their team to adopt a similar mindset toward self-improvement.

Inconsistencies, however, can quickly undermine this alignment. A leader who encourages risk-taking but penalizes failures sends conflicting messages, creating hesitation and diminishing trust. By contrast, a leader whose actions consistently support their words creates an environment where employees feel confident to act decisively and creatively.

Reinforcing Expectations and Norms

Consistent actions act as reinforcements for the cultural norms leaders aim to establish. Over time, repeated behaviors become ingrained in the team's operational fabric. A leader who practices open communication during critical meetings, for example, establishes a norm where transparency and dialogue become routine. Similarly, consistently recognizing individual contributions fosters an expectation of acknowledgment and mutual respect among team members.

This reinforcement is particularly valuable during times of change or uncertainty. Teams often look to leaders for cues on how to navigate disruptions. A leader who maintains composure, adheres to established values, and supports the team through challenges can help stabilize morale and build collective resilience.

Challenges of Staying Consistent

Remaining consistent as a leader can be difficult, especially in the face of external pressures and internal constraints. Decision fatigue, for instance, can lead to lapses in judgment or shifts in priorities. When leaders are overwhelmed with responsibilities, they may inadvertently send mixed signals, such as enforcing a work-life balance policy while overworking themselves or their teams.

External factors, such as shifting organizational priorities or market demands, also test a leader's ability to stay consistent. For instance, a sudden push for increased productivity might conflict with a long-standing emphasis on employee well-being. Navigating such dilemmas requires thoughtful prioritization and a commitment to core values.

Strategies for Consistency

To overcome these challenges, leaders can adopt several strategies:

1. Clarify Core Values: Leaders should clearly define their guiding principles and ensure these values serve as a foundation for decision-making and behavior.
2. Build Accountability Systems: Regular feedback loops and performance reviews can help leaders stay aligned with their own standards and identify areas for improvement.
3. Manage Energy Levels: Addressing decision fatigue through delegation, time management, and self-care can help leaders maintain focus and consistency.
4. Communicate Intentions: When deviations from norms are unavoidable, leaders should transparently communicate the reasons behind their actions to minimize confusion or mistrust.

6.1.3. Modeling Desired Behaviors in Practice

Leadership is most impactful when demonstrated through consistent, deliberate actions. Words may communicate intent, but it is through behavior that leaders truly influence team culture and expectations. By modeling the standards they wish to see, leaders not only set a clear example but also inspire their teams to embody those same qualities in their work.

The Power of Specific Behaviors

Certain behaviors, when demonstrated by leaders, act as tangible examples of team values:

1. Collaboration: When leaders actively engage in teamwork—soliciting input, sharing credit, and

offering support—they signal that collaboration is valued. A leader who actively participates in problem-solving or strategy discussions shows that every voice matters, encouraging others to contribute freely.
2. Punctuality: A leader who values timeliness by showing up prepared and on time for meetings sets a standard for professionalism. This action, though simple, conveys respect for others' time and establishes an expectation of accountability.
3. Ethical Decision-Making: Ethical leadership is vital in building trust and a sense of fairness. Leaders who consistently choose integrity over convenience, even in challenging situations, send a strong message about the importance of doing what is right over what is easy.

Examples of Behavior Shaping Team Culture

- Promoting Collaboration: At a design firm, a manager made it a point to participate in brainstorming sessions, emphasizing that innovative ideas often emerge from diverse perspectives. Their active involvement motivated team members to engage more openly, ultimately fostering a culture of creativity and shared ownership.
- Championing Punctuality: In a logistics company, a department head consistently started and ended meetings on time. This habit not only streamlined productivity but also encouraged team members to adopt similar practices, reducing delays across projects.

> Upholding Ethical Standards: At a tech startup, a CEO chose to delay a product launch to address a minor but potentially impactful bug. While the decision had short-term costs, it reinforced the company's commitment to quality and customer trust, earning respect from both employees and clients.

Practical Tips for Leaders to Model Behaviors

> Be Visible: Show your team that you are actively engaged and invested in their success. Attend critical team meetings, participate in decision-making processes, and be accessible.
> Celebrate What You Value: Recognize and reward behaviors that align with team goals and values, such as innovation, teamwork, or resilience.
> Demonstrate Commitment to Growth: Show your team that you are continuously striving to improve by staying updated on best practices, embracing new approaches, and adapting your behavior to meet evolving team needs. This proactive approach reinforces a culture of learning and progress.

6.2. Humility as a Leadership Superpower

Leadership often conjures images of unwavering authority, bold decision-making, and commanding confidence. Yet, amidst these traits lies a quality that is less conspicuous but equally, if not more, powerful—humility. Humility as a leadership attribute is neither about self-deprecation nor a lack of confidence. Rather, it represents a deep awareness of one's limitations, an openness to learning from others, and a genuine appreciation for the collective contributions of the team. Leaders who embrace humility not only build stronger connections with their teams but also create environments where collaboration and innovation thrive. In a world that constantly evolves, the humility to acknowledge the need for change, adapt, and seek input is no longer a luxury—it's a necessity.

Humility fosters a sense of trust and respect. A leader who is willing to admit mistakes, recognize the expertise of others, and accept constructive feedback creates a culture where team members feel valued and empowered. This subchapter explores the multifaceted role humility plays in leadership, delves into how it enhances team dynamics, and offers practical strategies for balancing humility with confidence. By understanding humility's transformative power, leaders can strengthen their teams and cultivate an atmosphere of mutual respect and shared purpose.

The Power of Humility in Collaboration

At the heart of humility lies the recognition that no single person has all the answers. This mindset is crucial in collaborative environments, where diverse perspectives and collective expertise drive success. Leaders who exhibit humility actively seek input from their teams, fostering a sense of ownership and shared responsibility. They understand that collaboration is not a threat to authority but a pathway to better decisions and outcomes.

For example, consider a project manager overseeing a cross-functional team in a tech company. By inviting ideas from engineers, designers, and marketers, the manager demonstrates humility, signaling that every voice matters. This approach not only enriches the project with varied insights but also motivates team members, who feel their contributions are genuinely valued.

Balancing Confidence with Humility

While humility is critical, it should not overshadow the confidence necessary for effective leadership. The key lies in balance. A leader must exude enough confidence to inspire trust and provide direction while maintaining the humility to acknowledge when they don't have all the answers. This balance is particularly important during high-pressure situations, where a leader's composure and openness can determine the team's ability to navigate challenges.

Practical ways to balance humility and confidence include:

- Acknowledging Expertise: Recognize team members' strengths and rely on their expertise where appropriate. This not only builds trust but also encourages team members to take initiative.
- Communicating Vision Clearly: Confidently articulate goals and expectations, ensuring the team understands the larger picture, even as you remain open to suggestions and adjustments.
- Embracing Vulnerability: Share personal challenges or lessons learned to demonstrate that growth is a continuous journey, regardless of one's position.

Strengthening Team Dynamics through Humility

Humility directly influences how leaders interact with their teams, creating a foundation for trust, respect, and collaboration. When leaders are humble, they:

1. Encourage Open Dialogue: By listening more than speaking, humble leaders create a safe space for team members to share ideas, concerns, and feedback.
2. Promote Mutual Respect: Humility fosters an environment where team members respect each other's contributions, breaking down silos and building stronger connections.
3. Model Accountability: A leader who admits mistakes demonstrates accountability, setting a standard for the entire team to own their actions.

These behaviors not only strengthen interpersonal relationships but also contribute to a culture where everyone feels empowered to contribute their best work.

Practical Steps to Cultivate Humility

Leaders can actively develop and demonstrate humility through intentional practices:

- Actively Listen: Prioritize listening to understand rather than to respond. This involves giving team members full attention and valuing their perspectives.
- Show Gratitude: Acknowledge and celebrate team achievements, highlighting the collective effort rather than taking personal credit.

- Seek Diverse Perspectives: Surround yourself with individuals who challenge your thinking and provide alternative viewpoints.
- Lead by Example: Exhibit humility in interactions, whether it's seeking feedback, crediting others for successes, or admitting when you're wrong.

The Long-Term Impact of Humility

The ripple effects of humility extend far beyond immediate team dynamics. A humble leader sets the tone for the entire organization, fostering a culture of respect, continuous learning, and innovation. Over time, this approach builds a resilient team that not only performs well but also thrives in the face of challenges.

Embracing humility, leaders can unlock their team's full potential, strengthen their own leadership effectiveness, and leave a lasting legacy of collaborative success. Humility, when paired with confidence and strategic action, becomes more than a leadership trait—it becomes a superpower.

6.3. Transparency and Open Communication

Transparency and open communication form the backbone of any thriving team. These elements are not just about sharing information; they are about building trust, strengthening relationships, and fostering a culture where everyone feels valued and informed. Leaders who prioritize transparency create an environment where employees are empowered to perform their best, knowing they are part of a team that values honesty and clarity. In a workplace, where uncertainty or miscommunication can easily lead to confusion or distrust, transparent leadership ensures alignment between the team's goals and actions.

Effective communication requires more than just disseminating information; it demands active listening, empathy, and a commitment to ensuring that all voices are heard. Transparency means being clear about decisions, challenges, and expectations, while also being open to feedback and collaboration. Leaders who excel in this area balance the need to share critical information with the awareness that overloading their team can be counterproductive. In this subchapter, we'll explore how open communication strengthens relationships, practical strategies to maintain transparency, and tools leaders can use to share information effectively without overwhelming their team.

The Role of Open Communication in Building Trust

Trust is the foundation of any successful team, and open communication is the key to building it. When leaders are transparent about their decisions and actions, they demonstrate respect for their team's intelligence and commitment. For example, instead of issuing a directive without context, a transparent leader explains the reasoning behind the decision, allowing team members to understand its importance and relevance. This approach not only fosters trust but also encourages team members to contribute their own insights and ideas.

Moreover, open communication helps to eliminate ambiguity. When team members know where they stand, what is expected of them, and the challenges the organization is facing, they are more likely to engage meaningfully with their work. Conversely, a lack of communication can breed uncertainty, leading to reduced morale and productivity. Leaders who prioritize transparency strengthen their team's resilience, as employees feel confident in their roles and the organization's direction.

Balancing Transparency with Clarity

While transparency is essential, leaders must avoid overwhelming their teams with excessive or irrelevant information. Over-communication can lead to confusion and frustration, particularly if employees feel inundated with details that do not directly impact their roles. Effective leaders know how to strike a balance—sharing enough information to keep their teams informed and engaged while filtering out unnecessary noise.

For example, during a significant organizational change, a leader might choose to provide high-level updates to the entire team while delegating more specific details to department heads. This approach ensures that everyone is aligned on the overall goals while allowing individual team members to focus on the information most relevant to them.

Tools and Techniques for Effective Transparency

Several tools and techniques can help leaders maintain transparency and facilitate open communication:

1. Regular Team Meetings: Holding consistent team meetings provides a platform to share updates, discuss challenges, and celebrate successes. These

meetings also allow team members to ask questions and voice concerns.
2. Open-Door Policies: An open-door policy encourages employees to approach leaders with their thoughts or issues, fostering a culture of openness and approachability.
3. Clear Documentation: Providing written updates or reports ensures that everyone has access to accurate information. Tools like project management software or shared dashboards can centralize communication and keep teams aligned.
4. Feedback Loops: Establishing regular feedback mechanisms—such as surveys, one-on-one check-ins, or suggestion boxes—demonstrates a leader's willingness to listen and adapt based on input from the team.
5. Transparency in Decision-Making: Sharing the thought process behind decisions, even when the outcomes are not favorable to all, builds trust. Leaders can explain how decisions align with organizational goals and why certain trade-offs were necessary.

The Ripple Effect of Transparent Leadership

Transparency not only strengthens relationships within the team but also enhances the organization's overall culture. Employees who feel informed and respected are more likely to become ambassadors of the company's values, contributing to a positive workplace environment. Furthermore, a culture of open communication can lead to greater innovation, as team members feel confident sharing ideas and collaborating without fear of judgment.

Ultimately, transparency and open communication are not just leadership tactics; they are reflections of a leader's commitment to fostering trust, clarity, and mutual respect within their team. Leaders who embrace these principles create a foundation for long-term success, enabling their teams to thrive even in the face of challenges.

6.4. Fostering Purpose and Meaning

In every organization, the most inspired and engaged teams are those that see their work as more than a series of tasks—they view it as contributing to something meaningful. The sense of purpose transforms a job into a mission, and it is the leader's role to help their team discover this connection. By aligning daily responsibilities with a larger vision, leaders can unlock a deeper level of commitment and motivation within their teams, fostering engagement that goes beyond mere productivity.

Purpose is not just a lofty concept; it is a driver of tangible outcomes. Employees who understand how their contributions impact the organization and society at large are more likely to feel invested in their work. In this subchapter, we will explore how leaders can create a culture of purpose by defining a clear vision, connecting individual roles to organizational goals, and celebrating the meaningful contributions of each team member.

The Role of Purpose in Leadership

Purpose is the "why" that fuels a leader's vision. A compelling purpose not only unites a team but also provides clarity in decision-making and direction. For example, in healthcare organizations, the purpose might be improving lives, while in a tech company, it could be innovation that changes how people interact with the world. Whatever the context, a leader's ability to articulate and embody this purpose sets the tone for the entire team.

Purpose-driven leadership fosters resilience during challenging times. When employees understand the value of their work, they are more likely to persevere in the face of obstacles. A leader who effectively communicates purpose turns setbacks into opportunities for reaffirming the mission, keeping morale and momentum high even in difficult circumstances.

Connecting Individual Roles to the Bigger Picture

A key aspect of fostering purpose is helping team members see how their specific roles contribute to the organization's broader goals. Employees who understand the "why" behind their tasks are more likely to approach their work with enthusiasm and creativity.

1. Clarify Organizational Goals: Start by ensuring the team has a clear understanding of the organization's mission and objectives. For instance, if the company's goal is to reduce environmental impact, leaders should articulate how individual roles—whether in production, marketing, or customer service—align with this vision.
2. Personalize the Impact: Go beyond general statements to highlight specific ways employees' work makes a difference. A customer service representative, for example, is not just resolving

complaints but also building lasting relationships that enhance customer loyalty and trust.
3. Provide Context During Transitions: In times of change, it's particularly important to reiterate how the team's efforts are helping the organization adapt and thrive. This helps employees feel included and valued even amid uncertainty.

Strategies to Foster Engagement and Meaning

To embed purpose into the team culture, leaders must actively create opportunities for meaningful engagement:

1. Celebrate Successes: Regularly recognize and celebrate the team's achievements, particularly those that align with the organization's mission. Public acknowledgment reinforces the idea that their efforts matter.
2. Encourage Skill Development: Helping employees grow professionally demonstrates that their potential is valued. A well-trained and confident employee is not only more effective but also more likely to find meaning in their work.
3. Foster Autonomy: Allowing team members the freedom to make decisions and innovate in their roles creates a sense of ownership. When employees feel trusted, they are more likely to align their work with the organization's purpose.
4. Facilitate Open Dialogues: Create opportunities for employees to discuss how their work ties into larger goals. Regular team discussions or one-on-one conversations can provide valuable insights and ensure everyone feels aligned and heard.

The Multiplier Effect of Purpose

When leaders successfully connect their team's work to a meaningful purpose, the benefits ripple outward. Engaged employees tend to be more collaborative, innovative, and resilient. This cultural shift can transform an organization, making it not only more successful but also a place where people feel proud to work.

Moreover, a purpose-driven culture attracts like-minded talent, creating a virtuous cycle of motivation and growth. As leaders invest in fostering meaning, they leave a legacy of empowerment, ensuring that their teams remain motivated and aligned with the organization's mission for years to come.

In essence, fostering purpose and meaning is about showing people that their work is not just about hitting targets—it's about making an impact. Leaders who embrace this responsibility inspire their teams to strive for greatness, turning ordinary efforts into extraordinary outcomes.

6.5. The Ripple Effect of Authentic Leadership

Authentic leadership has a profound and far-reaching influence, especially in the industrial sector, where operational excellence depends heavily on trust, collaboration, and shared vision. Beyond its immediate effects on team dynamics, authentic leadership creates a cascading impact that shapes organizational culture and inspires a new generation of leaders. The industrial context provides a unique backdrop where authenticity becomes a key differentiator in driving long-term success.

Cultivating a Trust-Based Culture

Authentic leaders in industrial environments are instrumental in building a culture rooted in trust and respect. By consistently aligning their actions with their values, these leaders demonstrate reliability and integrity, which encourages employees to do the same. In an industry where safety, efficiency, and quality are non-negotiable, a trust-based culture ensures that employees feel empowered to report issues, share innovative ideas, and take ownership of their roles without fear of criticism or retaliation.

For example, a factory manager who openly discusses both successes and challenges fosters an atmosphere of transparency that motivates the team to collaborate toward shared goals. Employees are more likely to embrace quality control measures, adhere to safety protocols, and actively contribute to continuous improvement initiatives when they see their leader exemplifying these principles.

Inspiring Leadership at All Levels

Authentic leadership inspires others to adopt similar values and behaviors, creating a ripple effect that extends throughout the organization. When leaders exhibit humility, resilience, and ethical decision-making, they serve as role models for their teams. In turn, employees who witness these qualities often emulate them in their interactions, gradually elevating the entire organization's culture.

This is particularly vital in industrial sectors, where leaders at every level—from line supervisors to executives—play a pivotal role in sustaining productivity and innovation. Leaders who are willing to mentor emerging talent, provide clear development pathways, and share their own leadership lessons instill confidence and ambition in the next generation of industry professionals.

Driving Organizational Resilience

Industries often face periods of disruption, whether due to technological advancements, supply chain challenges, or evolving market demands. Authentic leaders help their organizations navigate such challenges by fostering resilience and adaptability within their teams. By acknowledging uncertainties, involving the workforce in problem-solving, and maintaining open communication, these leaders create a stable yet flexible environment capable of withstanding shifts in the industrial landscape.

For instance, during a machinery upgrade in a manufacturing plant, authentic leadership ensures that employees are informed about changes, trained on new equipment, and given a platform to voice concerns. This approach not only minimizes resistance but also encourages employees to actively contribute to the transition's success.

Creating a Legacy of Authenticity

The most enduring impact of authentic leadership lies in its ability to create a legacy. Leaders who prioritize authenticity leave behind an organizational culture where honesty, collaboration, and accountability are deeply ingrained. In industrial settings, this legacy translates into higher employee retention, greater innovation, and a reputation for operational excellence that attracts top talent and loyal clients.

Authentic leaders invest in people, processes, and principles that outlast their tenure. They focus on shaping environments where future leaders can thrive—individuals who will carry forward the same values of integrity and trust, ensuring the organization's ongoing success.

Conclusion

The ripple effect of authentic leadership in the industrial world extends beyond immediate teams and operational outcomes. It reshapes organizational culture, inspires the next generation of leaders, and equips companies to adapt and excel in the face of challenges. Leading with authenticity, industrial leaders not only achieve sustainable success but also leave a legacy that empowers people and organizations to reach new heights.

6.6. Case Study 1: From Challenges to Triumph: How Authentic Leadership Transformed Best ClothingXYZ

Background
Best ClothingXYZ, one of Asia's largest apparel manufacturers, was a dominant player in the global market for over two decades. Known for its efficient operations and ability to deliver massive orders to retail giants worldwide, the company seemed unshakeable in its success. However, challenges began to mount as labor

dynamics shifted, customer expectations evolved, and technology-driven competitors entered the market.

The company's once-reliable operational model—focused on cost leadership and high-volume production—was no longer sufficient. Employee engagement dropped as workers struggled with repetitive tasks and felt disconnected from the company's goals. Leadership turnover compounded the problem, creating a perception of instability. The company needed a unifying vision and a leader capable of aligning its workforce with a clear purpose.

When Philip Duskbane took over as CEO, he faced the daunting challenge of restoring morale, modernizing operations, and re-establishing Best ClothingXYZ's position as a market leader.

Philip's Leadership Approach

Philip believed that authenticity, consistency, and an unrelenting focus on execution were critical to reigniting the company's momentum. His strategy revolved around redefining leadership at every level, making employees active participants in the company's transformation, and integrating technology to improve efficiency without losing the human touch.

1. Building a Culture of Ownership and Accountability

Philip began by revamping the company's leadership philosophy. He insisted that every leader—whether managing a factory line or a corporate division—

demonstrate the same level of accountability they expected from their teams.

To reinforce this principle, he initiated the "Own It Program," a framework designed to empower employees at every level to take ownership of their roles. Factory workers were given autonomy to identify inefficiencies in their workflows and propose solutions, while managers were encouraged to engage directly with their teams to understand challenges on the ground.

For example, a mid-level manager in the production department identified a bottleneck in the quality-check process that was delaying shipments. Encouraged by the "Own It Program," she collaborated with her team to redesign the workflow, cutting delays by 20%. Her initiative was recognized at a company-wide forum, further motivating others to think innovatively.

2. Leveraging Technology for Operational Excellence

Philip understood that to remain competitive, Best ClothingXYZ needed to modernize its operations. However, he also recognized the fears employees harbored about automation replacing jobs. To address this, Philip adopted a transparent approach, explaining how technology would be used to enhance rather than eliminate roles.

The company implemented "Smart Workflow Systems" across its factories, integrating AI and machine learning to optimize production schedules and reduce waste. Workers were trained to operate and troubleshoot the new systems, ensuring they were part of the technological transition.

This approach not only improved productivity but also reduced employee anxiety about job security. Factory workers began to see technology as a tool that empowered them to perform better and achieve more.

3. Connecting Employees to the Company's Vision

Philip believed that employees needed a reason to care beyond their daily tasks. He introduced a new mission statement for Best ClothingXYZ: "Clothing the world with excellence and pride."

To make this vision tangible, Philip launched an initiative where employees could participate in customer feedback sessions. Factory workers and designers attended virtual meetings with retail clients, gaining firsthand insights into how their work impacted the end consumer. This connection fostered a sense of pride and purpose across the workforce.

One memorable moment occurred when a factory worker in Bangladesh heard a retail executive praise the durability of a product line made in her facility. Tearing up, she shared how this acknowledgment inspired her to work with greater attention to detail. Stories like these spread across the organization, reinforcing a shared sense of purpose.

4. Balancing Innovation with People-Centric Leadership

While Philip focused on operational efficiency and modernization, he never lost sight of the human element. Recognizing that employees needed to feel valued during times of change, he launched a "Leadership at Every Level" initiative. This program identified high-potential employees in all departments and provided them with mentoring, cross-functional training, and opportunities to lead small-scale projects.

For example, a junior technician was given the chance to lead a project to redesign the factory's break room to improve worker satisfaction. The experience not only boosted her confidence but also set a precedent for grassroots leadership within the company.

Outcomes of Authentic Leadership

Philip's leadership approach produced remarkable results:

1. Increased Productivity: The introduction of Smart Workflow Systems reduced production errors by 30% and increased on-time delivery rates to 98%.
2. Enhanced Employee Engagement: Employee satisfaction surveys showed a 70% improvement within three years, and turnover rates dropped significantly.
3. Market Competitiveness: Best ClothingXYZ regained its position as a preferred supplier for top retailers, securing long-term contracts worth billions.

Philip's ability to align his actions with his vision transformed the company's culture, operations, and market standing. His leadership inspired employees to see themselves as integral to Best ClothingXYZ's success, creating a ripple effect that continues to shape the organization's future.

6.7. Case Study 2: From Stagnation to Innovation: The Leadership Journey of Elisabeth Emberhall

Work MachineryXYZ, one of the largest manufacturers of heavy industrial equipment in the United States, had long been an industry leader known for its high-quality machinery and innovative solutions. However, as the market evolved toward automation and smart technologies, the company began to face a period of stagnation. Internally, morale dipped due to unclear communication from leadership, leaving employees feeling disconnected from the company's mission.

When Elisabeth Emberhall stepped in as CEO, she was faced with a dual challenge: reignite innovation and rebuild trust across the organization. Elisabeth, known for her authentic and people-centered leadership, took a proactive approach to unite the workforce and steer the company toward a renewed vision of success.

Step 1: Rebuilding Trust Through Transparent Leadership

Elisabeth recognized that transparency was crucial in earning the trust of employees, many of whom felt left out of strategic conversations. She initiated a company-wide "open door" policy, emphasizing accessibility at all levels of leadership. Additionally, Elisabeth began hosting monthly town halls to openly discuss company performance, challenges, and future plans.

In her first town hall, she addressed the elephant in the room: the company's lag in adapting to industry trends. Rather than assigning blame, Elisabeth focused on the collective opportunity to modernize and innovate, asking employees to actively participate in shaping the company's future.

By openly acknowledging the company's challenges and inviting solutions, Elisabeth set a precedent for honesty and collaboration, laying the foundation for cultural transformation.

Step 2: Aligning Work with a Purposeful Vision

To combat the sense of disconnection within the workforce, Elisabeth worked to redefine the company's mission and tie each employee's work to a larger purpose. She launched a new corporate initiative: *"Building Machinery That Builds the Future."* This vision highlighted the company's critical role in enabling infrastructure, manufacturing, and energy industries to innovate and thrive.

Elisabeth made it a priority to highlight the impact of employees' contributions. For instance, she shared stories of how Work MachineryXYZ's equipment had been used in constructing sustainable energy plants and rebuilding disaster-hit areas. These narratives became a powerful motivator, helping employees understand that their daily efforts went beyond the factory floor—they were shaping lives and industries.

Step 3: Fostering Collaboration and Recognition

Elisabeth quickly realized that Work MachineryXYZ's departmental silos were a significant barrier to innovation. She introduced collaborative task forces that included employees from diverse backgrounds—engineers, production staff, and customer support teams—to develop solutions for key challenges. One notable example was the creation of a "Rapid Innovation Lab" where cross-functional teams worked on prototypes for smart machinery in real time.

To further strengthen the culture of collaboration, Elisabeth implemented a recognition program that celebrated teamwork and values-driven performance. This program emphasized not just output but also behaviors like mentorship, creative problem-solving, and knowledge sharing.

Step 4: Leading by Example

Elisabeth's leadership style was grounded in action, not just words. She frequently visited production facilities and engaged with employees across all levels, ensuring her presence was both visible and meaningful. During one visit, she personally joined a quality control team to better understand the day-to-day challenges faced on the assembly line.

Her commitment to consistency extended beyond interpersonal interactions. For instance, when cost-cutting measures became necessary, Elisabeth made a point of protecting jobs and instead focused on streamlining processes. By prioritizing the well-being of employees, she demonstrated the values of fairness and integrity that she advocated for the entire organization.

Step 5: Outcomes and Legacy

Elisabeth Emberhall's leadership transformed Work MachineryXYZ in profound ways. Within three years, the company launched its first line of fully automated smart machinery, which quickly became a market leader. Employee engagement scores rose by 40%, and turnover decreased significantly, a testament to the renewed sense of purpose within the workforce.

The cultural shift Elisabeth spearheaded also had ripple effects beyond immediate results. She inspired a new generation of leaders within the company who embraced her principles of transparency, collaboration, and purpose-driven leadership. As these leaders rose through the ranks, they continued to build on Elisabeth's foundation, ensuring that Work MachineryXYZ's legacy of excellence would endure.

Key Takeaways

Elisabeth Emberhall's tenure at Work MachineryXYZ underscores the transformative power of authentic leadership in the industrial sector. By prioritizing transparency, aligning work with purpose, and fostering collaboration, Elisabeth not only revitalized a company but also empowered its people to believe in their collective potential. Her story is a powerful reminder that great leaders shape organizations by investing in their culture and people, leaving a legacy that extends well beyond their tenure.

Chapter 7: From Good to Great Leadership

Leadership is not a static skill but a dynamic journey that evolves with experience, reflection, and the challenges faced along the way. Moving from being a competent leader to a truly great one requires more than mastering the basics—it demands a relentless commitment to growth, a willingness to embrace change, and an unwavering focus on the success of others. Great leaders are those who transform their teams and organizations by fostering innovation, inspiring trust, and creating an environment where individuals feel empowered to excel. This journey from good to great is not defined by titles or accolades but by the tangible and lasting impact a leader leaves behind.

The path to exceptional leadership is built on continuous improvement. It requires leaders to cultivate self-awareness, seek constructive feedback, and adapt their strategies to meet the evolving needs of their teams and industries. Equally important is the ability to measure progress—both personal and organizational—through meaningful metrics that go beyond financial results. True greatness in leadership is about more than achieving immediate goals; it's about leaving a legacy that endures, inspiring others to carry forward the values, vision, and excellence established under your guidance.

In this chapter, we will explore the key elements that distinguish great leaders from good ones. From fostering a culture of continuous improvement to self-reflection, feedback, and the measurement of success, this chapter will provide practical strategies for elevating your leadership to the next level. Finally, we will discuss the legacy of leadership—how great leaders inspire future generations and leave an indelible mark on their organizations and industries.

7.1. The Evolution of Leadership: From Competence to Excellence

Leadership is not a static attribute but a dynamic journey that unfolds over time. It begins with competence—a solid foundation of knowledge, skills, and the ability to perform well in a given role. However, competence alone does not define great leadership. To move from good to great, leaders must embrace the idea of continuous evolution, adapting to new challenges, fostering innovation, and developing a deeper connection with their teams. This progression requires a mindset shift: from focusing solely on individual performance to driving collective success and long-term impact.

In today's fast-paced industrial landscape, adaptability and resilience have become essential traits. Leaders are no longer just tasked with meeting targets but also with navigating uncharted territories such as technological disruptions, global supply chain challenges, and evolving employee expectations. This shift demands a broader vision, one that prioritizes agility, growth, and collaboration. Great leaders recognize that their ability to evolve is directly tied to their willingness to learn from experience, accept feedback, and adjust their strategies in response to a changing environment.

Leadership Evolution Through Experience

Every leader's journey begins with foundational competencies—mastering technical skills, understanding the organizational framework, and building relationships with peers and subordinates. These competencies are crucial for establishing credibility. However, as leaders take on greater responsibilities, their focus must shift toward more complex objectives, such as shaping organizational culture, influencing external stakeholders, and inspiring innovation.

One hallmark of leadership excellence is the ability to transform setbacks into opportunities for growth. Great leaders view failures not as dead ends but as valuable learning experiences that refine their decision-making abilities. For instance, a manager in a manufacturing plant who encounters delays due to equipment malfunctions might use the experience to implement preventive maintenance systems, avoiding future disruptions while enhancing operational efficiency.

Adaptability: The Key to Sustained Growth

Adaptability is the bridge that connects competence to excellence. It enables leaders to respond effectively to changing circumstances without losing sight of their vision. In the industrial sector, for example, the rapid adoption of automation and artificial intelligence has transformed workflows and required leaders to rethink traditional management approaches. Those who adapt by embracing new technologies and upskilling their teams demonstrate not only competence but also forward-thinking leadership.

An adaptable leader is also open to diverse perspectives, recognizing that innovation often emerges from collaboration across functions and hierarchies. By fostering an environment where team members feel empowered to share ideas and take initiative, leaders can drive continuous improvement and maintain a competitive edge.

The Leadership Growth Mindset

At the heart of leadership evolution lies a mindset focused on growth and adaptation. Leaders who prioritize ongoing development—whether through mentorship, formal education, or active participation in industry networks—demonstrate their dedication to both personal and professional excellence. By committing to this mindset, they not only enhance their own capabilities but also inspire their teams to embrace learning as a core value.

Self-awareness is another key pillar of this mindset. Leaders who understand their strengths and areas for improvement are better equipped to make strategic decisions and foster meaningful relationships. This self-knowledge also encourages collaboration, as it enables leaders to leverage their team's expertise rather than feeling the need to have all the answers.

Humility plays an integral role as well. A leader's willingness to acknowledge gaps in knowledge and seek input from others creates an environment of trust and inclusivity. When combined with a growth-oriented approach, this humility empowers teams to take ownership of their contributions and aim for higher levels of performance. Together, these traits define a leadership style that evolves with the times while inspiring collective progress.

Setting the Stage for Greatness

As leaders progress from competence to excellence, they become architects of a culture that prioritizes growth, innovation, and resilience. They recognize that leadership is not about individual accolades but about fostering an environment where the organization and its people can thrive. By continuously evolving and adapting, leaders not only enhance their own effectiveness but also create a lasting legacy of success and impact.

7.2. Building a Culture of Continuous Improvement

Continuous improvement is the heartbeat of a thriving organization. It embodies the commitment to consistently refine processes, enhance performance, and exceed expectations. Leaders play a pivotal role in shaping this culture by fostering a mindset of growth and innovation within their teams. A culture of continuous improvement isn't just about incremental gains—it's about creating a dynamic environment where employees feel empowered to experiment, innovate, and pursue excellence.

Establishing the Foundation for Growth

The first step in building a culture of continuous improvement is creating an environment where learning and experimentation are valued over fear of failure. Leaders must clearly articulate the organization's vision for improvement, tying it to overarching business objectives. When employees understand how their efforts contribute to larger goals, they are more likely to take ownership of their work and seek ways to improve.

An effective strategy is to integrate continuous improvement into the organization's core values. For example, a company specializing in heavy machinery manufacturing might adopt principles such as lean manufacturing or Six Sigma. These methodologies not only streamline operations but also instill a mindset of constant evaluation and enhancement across all levels of the organization.

Empowering Employees to Innovate

At the heart of continuous improvement is employee empowerment. When individuals feel trusted and supported, they are more inclined to identify inefficiencies, suggest creative solutions, and take initiative. Leaders can encourage this by:

1. Providing Autonomy: Allow employees to take ownership of their projects and make decisions within their scope of work. This autonomy fosters a sense of responsibility and pride in their contributions.
2. Investing in Skill Development: Equip employees with the tools and training they need to excel. Offering upskilling programs, workshops, and cross-functional training helps bridge skill gaps and enables teams to tackle challenges with confidence.
3. Recognizing Contributions: Celebrate achievements and acknowledge those who drive positive change. Publicly recognizing innovative ideas or successful

process improvements reinforces the importance of continuous improvement within the organization.

Encouraging a Feedback-Driven Environment

Feedback is the lifeblood of continuous improvement. Leaders must create mechanisms for gathering insights from employees, customers, and stakeholders. Open forums, suggestion boxes, and periodic team reviews provide opportunities for employees to voice concerns and propose ideas.

Moreover, leaders should model openness to feedback themselves, demonstrating that constructive criticism is a tool for growth, not a personal attack. This transparency encourages a two-way exchange of ideas, fostering trust and collaboration.

Addressing Change Challenges

While building a culture of continuous improvement is rewarding, it can also face resistance. Employees may feel overwhelmed by constant change or uncertain about how new processes will affect their roles. Leaders can address this resistance by:

1. Communicating Benefits Clearly: Explain how changes will improve workflows, enhance job satisfaction, or contribute to organizational success.
2. Starting Small: Implement incremental changes rather than overhauling systems overnight. Small

wins build momentum and demonstrate the value of improvement efforts.
3. Involving Employees Early: Engage employees in the decision-making process. When they are part of the conversation, they are more likely to embrace change and champion it among their peers.

Aligning Improvement Efforts with Business Goals

Continuous improvement should not occur in isolation; it must align with the organization's strategic objectives. Leaders must ensure that every initiative—whether it involves optimizing supply chains, enhancing customer experiences, or reducing production waste—serves a greater purpose. Regularly revisiting these goals and tracking progress ensures that efforts remain relevant and impactful.

The Role of Leadership in Sustaining Improvement

Leaders are the torchbearers of continuous improvement. Their commitment to growth sets the tone for the entire organization. By modeling behaviors such as adaptability, resilience, and curiosity, leaders inspire their teams to adopt the same mindset.

To sustain this culture, leaders must also remain vigilant against complacency. Periodic assessments of processes, technologies, and team dynamics help identify areas for enhancement, ensuring that improvement remains a constant pursuit.

Conclusion

Building a culture of continuous improvement transforms organizations into dynamic, forward-thinking entities. It fosters innovation, empowers employees, and drives business success. By aligning improvement efforts with strategic goals and cultivating an environment of trust and collaboration, leaders ensure that their teams are not only prepared for today's challenges but are also equipped to seize tomorrow's opportunities. This culture, championed by strong leadership, becomes a cornerstone of long-term excellence.

7.3. Self-Reflection and Feedback: The Pillars of Personal Development

Leadership development begins with self-awareness and a willingness to improve. This subchapter focuses on the transformative power of self-reflection and structured feedback in shaping exceptional leaders. By understanding one's strengths, recognizing blind spots, and adapting based on constructive input, leaders can continuously refine their skills and approach.

The Role of Self-Reflection in Leadership

Self-reflection is a foundational practice for effective leadership. Leaders who regularly assess their decisions, communication style, and emotional responses are better equipped to grow and adapt. This process involves asking introspective questions such as:

- Did I communicate my expectations clearly?
- How did my actions align with my stated values?

> What could I have done differently to achieve a better outcome?

In the industrial sector, where the stakes are high and change is constant, reflective practices allow leaders to anticipate challenges, learn from failures, and replicate successful strategies. A leader who pauses to evaluate not only their decisions but also the dynamics of their team gains valuable insights into how to steer their organization toward success.

Leveraging Feedback as a Growth Tool

Feedback is often regarded as a mirror for leadership effectiveness. Constructive input from peers, team members, and mentors can uncover blind spots that self-reflection alone may miss. Effective leaders proactively seek feedback through:

> - 360-Degree Reviews: Comprehensive evaluations from superiors, peers, and subordinates offer a holistic view of a leader's performance.
> - Mentorship Programs: Engaging with mentors provides guidance based on real-world experience and allows for candid discussions about growth areas.
> - Anonymous Surveys: Anonymous feedback from team members can yield honest, actionable insights that might not surface in face-to-face interactions.

Acting on feedback is equally crucial. Leaders who incorporate this input into their strategies demonstrate adaptability and a commitment to personal development, inspiring their teams to embrace continuous improvement as well.

Creating Personal Development Plans

To maximize the value of self-reflection and feedback, leaders should formalize their growth efforts with personal development plans (PDPs). A well-structured PDP includes:

1. Clear Goals: Objectives that align with the organization's needs and the leader's aspirations.
2. Actionable Steps: Specific, measurable actions to improve identified weaknesses or build on strengths.
3. Timelines: Defined periods for reassessment and progress tracking.
4. Accountability Mechanisms: Regular check-ins with mentors or peers to ensure progress.

For example, an industrial leader striving to improve communication might set a goal to hold biweekly team briefings, solicit feedback on their clarity, and review progress after three months.

The Transformative Impact

When leaders engage in self-reflection and actively seek feedback, they not only improve their individual effectiveness but also set an example for their teams. This culture of openness and growth fosters trust, accountability, and resilience—qualities that drive organizations to excel in competitive markets.

7.4. Metrics of Leadership Success: Measuring What Matters

Leadership success is often perceived as intangible, a combination of charisma, decision-making prowess, and influence. However, in industrial environments, where outcomes must align with measurable objectives, it becomes critical to define and quantify what successful leadership looks like. Leaders need clear benchmarks—not only for their growth but to ensure their teams and organizations thrive. This subchapter delves into the critical dimensions of assessing leadership, balancing tangible metrics with qualitative insights, and recognizing the broader cultural impact of effective leadership.

Tangible Metrics: Defining Success Through Results

1. Operational Excellence:
    - Leaders must look at measurable outcomes, such as production efficiency, reduced downtime, and adherence to project timelines. These indicators provide a direct link between leadership effectiveness and organizational results.
    - For example, in large machinery manufacturing, a leader who fosters collaboration between design and production teams might achieve faster time-to-market for new models, signaling operational success.
2. Employee Engagement and Retention Rates:
    - High engagement levels suggest a motivated workforce, reflecting the leader's ability to inspire and align the team's efforts

with organizational goals. Retention metrics, on the other hand, reveal whether employees feel valued and supported.
- Leaders can analyze patterns in employee turnover, comparing rates before and after implementing new leadership practices, to understand their influence on workplace stability.
3. Client and Stakeholder Satisfaction:
    - For industrial leaders, success is often mirrored in customer satisfaction and stakeholder trust. Metrics such as customer retention, net promoter scores, or stakeholder feedback are strong indicators of a leader's ability to meet or exceed expectations.

Intangible Indicators: Leadership's Cultural Impact

1. Trust and Team Cohesion:
    - A thriving team culture marked by trust and camaraderie is one of the strongest indicators of effective leadership. Leaders can gauge this through qualitative observations, such as how openly employees collaborate or express concerns.
    - A leader who actively listens to their team, involves them in decisions, and provides constructive feedback fosters a sense of belonging that no numerical metric can fully capture.
2. Innovation and Adaptability:
    - The presence of innovative ideas within a team is a hallmark of a leader who

empowers employees to think creatively and take risks. Successful leaders encourage adaptability, enabling teams to embrace change and respond effectively to challenges.
3. Reputation and Influence:
    - Beyond internal dynamics, leaders leave an impression on the broader community and industry. Indicators such as external recognition, industry accolades, or partnerships signify the leader's broader impact and credibility.

Alternative Methods of Measurement

1. Milestone Reviews:
    - Leaders can establish periodic milestone reviews to assess progress on long-term goals. These reviews encourage reflection on achievements and ensure alignment with strategic objectives.
2. Success Stories and Case Studies:
    - Examining specific instances where leadership made a difference—such as resolving a crisis or achieving a challenging goal—provides qualitative insights into effectiveness. These stories are valuable for identifying patterns in decision-making and leadership impact.
3. Cultural Assessments:
    - Conduct surveys and focus groups to evaluate the team's perception of the organizational culture and leadership

impact. Questions can explore themes such as inclusion, innovation, and trust.

Conclusion: Leadership as a Measurable Journey

While the art of leadership may seem intangible, its success leaves a clear trail of evidence—both measurable and cultural. Tangible results like operational efficiency and employee retention align with the organization's strategic goals, while intangible indicators such as innovation and trust reflect the depth of a leader's influence. By using a combination of metrics, leaders can continuously evaluate and refine their approach, ensuring their efforts drive sustainable success.

7.5. The Legacy of Leadership: Inspiring Future Generations

Leadership is more than guiding a team to meet immediate goals or achieve quarterly targets—it is about leaving a legacy that outlives the leader. In industrial environments, where organizations often face technological advancements, workforce transitions, and competitive pressures, a leader's influence must extend beyond their tenure. This subchapter explores how leaders can create a lasting impact by nurturing the next generation, embedding enduring values into organizational culture, and laying a foundation for sustainable success. Great leaders understand that their ultimate achievement is not measured by personal accolades but by the growth, resilience, and vision they instill in others.

Mentoring Emerging Leaders: Passing the Torch

1. The Role of Mentorship:
    - Mentorship bridges the gap between experience and potential. By guiding emerging leaders, seasoned executives ensure their expertise and insights are passed down, fostering continuity in leadership quality.
    - For example, leaders in the machinery manufacturing sector often mentor engineers transitioning into management roles, equipping them with strategic thinking and decision-making skills.
2. Identifying High-Potential Talent:
    - Legacy-focused leaders proactively identify team members with leadership potential. This involves observing not just technical competence but also interpersonal skills, problem-solving ability, and a willingness to learn.
    - By investing in formal training programs and shadowing opportunities, leaders help future managers gain the confidence and tools needed to excel.
3. Encouraging Autonomy and Growth:
    - Delegating responsibilities and encouraging emerging leaders to make decisions fosters their independence and critical thinking. This practice not only prepares them for future challenges but also instills trust in the leader's vision.

Embedding Values in Organizational Culture

1. Living the Values Daily:
    - Leaders who consistently embody organizational values—whether integrity, innovation, or collaboration—create a culture that aligns behavior with shared principles. Their actions set the tone for future leaders, who are more likely to internalize these values.
2. Formalizing the Legacy:
    - Codifying values into mission statements, training materials, and operational guidelines ensures they are preserved long after a leader's tenure. This practice helps sustain cultural coherence even during leadership transitions.
    - For example, leaders in global manufacturing firms often implement programs to celebrate achievements that align with core values, reinforcing their importance to the organization.
3. Building Resilience for the Future:
    - A strong cultural foundation prepares the organization to weather external disruptions and adapt to evolving demands. Leaders who emphasize resilience embed adaptability as a key value, ensuring their teams remain agile and resourceful.

Shaping the Next Generation of Leaders

1. Creating Leadership Pipelines:
   - Establishing structured development pathways, such as rotational programs or cross-functional assignments, equips employees with diverse experiences that prepare them for leadership roles.
   - For instance, leaders in industrial firms might design programs where employees spend time in different departments—engineering, procurement, and customer relations—to develop holistic perspectives.
2. Leading by Example:
   - Demonstrating qualities such as perseverance, ethical decision-making, and visionary thinking inspires emerging leaders to emulate these traits in their own careers.
   - A leader's ability to remain composed during crises and to act decisively under pressure becomes a blueprint for future leaders navigating their own challenges.
3. Celebrating Successors' Achievements:
   - A leader's true legacy is reflected in the accomplishments of those they mentored and guided. Recognizing and celebrating their growth reinforces the cycle of leadership development and motivates others to strive for excellence.

Conclusion: A Legacy Beyond Personal Achievements
The impact of a leader is not confined to their tenure but resonates through the people they inspire and the values they instill. By mentoring future leaders, embedding core

principles into organizational culture, and preparing teams for long-term success, leaders create a legacy that transcends their individual accomplishments. In doing so, they contribute to the sustainability of their industry and ensure that leadership excellence endures for generations to come.

7.6. Case Study 1: Mike's Leadership Revolution at Foods XYZ Co

In the competitive food manufacturing industry, the ability to adapt and innovate often separates thriving companies from those struggling to stay relevant. Foods XYZ Co, a leading global food producer, had enjoyed decades of success but recently found itself at a crossroads. Market dynamics were changing rapidly, driven by consumer demand for healthier, sustainably sourced options. Internally, the company grappled with inefficiencies, low employee morale, and a lack of innovation.

This is the story of how Mike, an exceptional leader, transformed Foods XYZ Co by turning leadership principles into action. His journey exemplifies how moving from good to great leadership can ripple through an organization, driving cultural shifts, innovation, and long-term growth.

The Crisis: Stagnation in a Changing Landscape
When Mike stepped into his role as CEO, Foods XYZ Co was facing challenges on multiple fronts. The company's traditional products were losing market share to startups with trendy, health-focused offerings. Moreover, operational silos prevented departments from collaborating effectively, stifling creativity and agility. Employee engagement surveys revealed widespread

dissatisfaction, with many workers feeling undervalued and uninspired.

Mike recognized that incremental changes wouldn't suffice. The company needed a leadership overhaul to align its vision, empower its workforce, and inspire innovation.

Mike's Leadership Approach

Mike's approach to leadership transformation was multifaceted and deeply rooted in the principles of adaptability, continuous improvement, and purpose-driven leadership.

1. Reimagining the Company's Vision
    - Mike believed that leadership begins with a compelling vision. He spearheaded a strategic planning initiative that involved employees at all levels. Through town hall meetings and brainstorming sessions, he gathered input and refined the company's mission: to create innovative, health-focused products while leading the industry in sustainability.
    - The new vision was not just a statement; it became a rallying cry that resonated with employees and consumers alike.
2. Fostering a Culture of Innovation
    - Mike encouraged teams to experiment and take calculated risks. He introduced "Innovation Days," where employees could pitch ideas for new products or process improvements.

- By creating an environment where failure was seen as a learning opportunity, Mike unlocked a wave of creativity. Within a year, the company launched a line of plant-based snacks that became a bestseller.
3. Empowering Employees
    - Recognizing that disengaged employees were a barrier to success, Mike revamped the company's approach to employee development. He introduced mentorship programs, upskilling initiatives, and leadership training workshops.
    - To ensure employees felt heard, he implemented regular feedback loops and anonymous suggestion platforms. These measures gave employees a sense of ownership and purpose, significantly boosting morale.
4. Operational Excellence and Collaboration
    - Mike addressed operational inefficiencies by breaking down silos. He restructured the organization into cross-functional teams that worked collaboratively on product development and process optimization.
    - This shift not only accelerated project timelines but also fostered a sense of camaraderie across departments.

Outcomes: Turning Vision into Reality

1. A Cultural Renaissance
    - Employees at Foods XYZ Co began to embody the company's redefined values. From factory workers to senior managers,

everyone aligned with Mike's emphasis on innovation, collaboration, and purpose.
- Employee engagement scores surged, reflecting a more motivated and connected workforce.

2. Market Leadership and Financial Growth
   - The introduction of innovative product lines allowed Foods XYZ Co to recapture market share. The plant-based snack division alone grew revenues by 40% in two years.
   - Sustainable practices not only reduced costs but also attracted eco-conscious consumers, further enhancing the brand's reputation.

3. A Legacy of Leadership Excellence
   - Mike's efforts to mentor emerging leaders bore fruit. Several protégés stepped into key leadership roles, ensuring that the principles of adaptability, purpose, and empowerment continued to guide the company.

Lessons in Leadership Excellence

Mike's journey offers profound insights into what it takes to evolve from good to great leadership:

1. Purpose as a Catalyst:
   - By redefining the company's mission, Mike inspired a shared sense of purpose that motivated employees and resonated with customers.

2. Empowerment and Ownership:
   - Giving employees the tools and opportunities to contribute meaningfully fosters a culture of innovation and accountability.
3. Long-Term Impact:
   - True leadership success lies not only in immediate results but also in the legacy of growth, resilience, and excellence that leaders leave behind.

Conclusion

Mike's transformation of Foods XYZ Co demonstrates how exceptional leadership can redefine an organization's trajectory. His ability to align vision with action, empower his team, and foster a culture of innovation underscores the principles explored in this chapter. Through his leadership, Foods XYZ Co not only regained its competitive edge but also set a benchmark for others to follow.

7.7. Case Study 2: Transforming Health Devices XYZ – From Industry Player to Innovator

In the highly competitive and regulated world of medical devices, Health Devices XYZ was a respected name but struggled with a reputation for being slow to adapt to new market demands. Despite a strong product line, the company faced increasing competition from more agile, technology-focused startups. Employee morale was waning, and innovation pipelines were lagging. That changed when Steven, a seasoned leader with a passion for excellence, took the helm.

Visionary Leadership Meets Industry Challenges

Steven's first move was to establish a clear, unifying vision: to make Health Devices XYZ not only a provider of high-quality products but a leader in groundbreaking medical innovations that improved patient care globally. His message resonated across the company, from the boardroom to the manufacturing floor.

However, vision alone wasn't enough. Steven knew that to drive change, he needed to address three critical areas: employee engagement, innovation processes, and organizational culture.

Building a Culture of Innovation and Empowerment

Steven introduced the "Innovation Sprint Program", a series of workshops and cross-functional projects designed to identify and accelerate promising ideas. Employees were encouraged to think beyond their traditional roles, resulting in collaborative breakthroughs. One such project led to the development of a wearable medical device that significantly improved patient monitoring, a product that became a flagship for the company.

To empower his team, Steven also revised the company's feedback structure. Recognizing the importance of transparent communication, he implemented biweekly town halls and anonymous suggestion platforms. These efforts created a culture where employees felt heard and valued, reigniting their passion for their work.

Strategic Risk-Taking

Another hallmark of Steven's leadership was his willingness to take calculated risks. Health Devices XYZ had long avoided entering the telemedicine market, fearing the complexities of integrating digital health platforms with their existing devices. Steven championed the exploration of this new frontier, investing in partnerships with tech firms to co-develop solutions.

This strategic pivot not only expanded the company's market presence but also positioned it as a leader in connected healthcare. Within three years, revenues from telemedicine-compatible devices accounted for 25% of the company's total income, significantly boosting its financial performance.

Mentoring Future Leaders

Steven understood that sustainable success depended on more than immediate results; it required a pipeline of capable leaders. He personally mentored a select group of high-potential employees, providing them with exposure to strategic decision-making processes.

One mentee, a rising star in the R&D department, later led a breakthrough project that reduced production costs by 15% without compromising quality—an achievement that further solidified Health Devices XYZ's competitive edge.

The Ripple Effect of Authentic Leadership

Steven's authentic leadership not only transformed the company's internal dynamics but also reshaped its reputation in the market. Clients and stakeholders increasingly viewed Health Devices XYZ as an agile, innovative partner rather than a traditional industry player.

By the end of Steven's fifth year as CEO, Health Devices XYZ had achieved:

- A 40% increase in annual revenue.
- Recognition as a top innovator in the medical devices industry by a leading trade publication.
- A 20% improvement in employee retention rates, reflecting the revitalized company culture.

Lessons for Aspiring Leaders

Steven's journey at Health Devices XYZ demonstrates that great leadership involves more than setting a vision—it requires the courage to disrupt the status quo, the humility to listen and adapt, and the foresight to invest in both people and innovation. Through his efforts, Steven not only turned Health Devices XYZ into an industry leader but also inspired a new generation of innovators to carry the company's legacy forward.

Conclusion: A Call to Action

Leadership is more than a title or position—it is a journey defined by continuous learning, self-reflection, and purposeful action. Throughout this book, we've explored the many dimensions of leadership, from understanding and connecting with your team to driving innovation, fostering resilience, and leaving a lasting legacy. Each chapter has uncovered a crucial piece of the puzzle, forming a comprehensive framework for aspiring leaders to not only excel but to inspire others to greatness.

At its core, leadership is about people. It's about recognizing that every individual on your team brings unique skills, perspectives, and aspirations to the table. It's about understanding their strengths, helping them overcome challenges, and guiding them toward shared goals. This human-centered approach is what distinguishes great leaders from good ones.

Reflect on Your Leadership Journey

As you turn the final pages of this book, take a moment to reflect on your own leadership journey. Ask yourself:

- How well do I understand my team's work and challenges?
- Am I fostering an environment where innovation thrives and risks are embraced?
- Do my actions align with my values, and do I model the behavior I expect from others?
- Am I leaving a legacy that inspires future generations to lead with authenticity and purpose?

Leadership is a lifelong process of growth. It requires humility to acknowledge where we fall short and courage to take action to improve. The best leaders aren't those who have all the answers but those who are willing to learn, adapt, and lead by example.

Take Action Today

Leadership isn't something you wait to master before practicing—it's a skill honed through action. Start small. Implement one idea from this book in your daily routine, whether it's scheduling a one-on-one meeting to understand a team member's aspirations, organizing a team-building activity, or reflecting on your own leadership style. Small changes, when done consistently, lead to transformative results.

Remember, leadership isn't just about achieving organizational goals. It's about creating a culture where individuals feel valued, empowered, and motivated to contribute their best. As you integrate these practices into your leadership, you'll not only see improvements in performance but also in trust, loyalty, and engagement within your team.

The Broader Impact of Leadership

The ripple effect of great leadership extends far beyond the workplace. By mentoring and empowering others, you contribute to a cycle of growth and development that strengthens your organization and community. The lessons you impart and the values you uphold have the power to shape not only your immediate team but also future leaders who will continue your legacy.

In a world that is constantly evolving, the need for adaptive, empathetic, and visionary leaders has never been greater. Industries are being transformed by technology, societal expectations are shifting, and the challenges leaders face are becoming increasingly complex. Yet, the principles of effective leadership remain timeless: empathy, authenticity, resilience, and a commitment to continuous improvement.

A Challenge to Lead Differently

As you move forward, challenge yourself to lead differently. Break free from outdated norms, embrace vulnerability, and inspire others through your actions. Leadership isn't about perfection—it's about progress. The most inspiring leaders are those who remain learners at heart, open to new ideas and dedicated to making a meaningful impact.

Let this book serve as a guide and a reminder that leadership is not a solitary pursuit. It's a shared endeavor that thrives on collaboration, mutual respect, and a shared vision. Together, as leaders committed to growth, innovation, and authenticity, we have the power to drive change and build a better future.

So, take the first step today. Reflect, adapt, and act with purpose. The journey from good to great leadership is not an easy one, but it is one of the most rewarding paths you can take. Lead boldly, inspire intentionally, and leave a legacy that makes a difference.

About The Author

Liviu Ghiuzan brings over 15 years of leadership experience, guiding professionals and organizations toward achieving excellence. With a proven track record in technical expertise, operational efficiency, and fostering collaborative work environments, he has worked closely with industry leaders and teams across diverse sectors.

Liviu is passionate about empowering leaders to bridge the gap between technical understanding and transformative leadership, helping them navigate challenges, inspire their teams, and drive meaningful change. His insights are rooted in years of hands-on experience, mentoring, and delivering tailored training programs designed to cultivate effective leadership practices.

Through his work, Liviu continues to inspire leaders to embrace innovation, build resilience, and lead with purpose. Connect with him on LinkedIn to join the conversation: https://www.linkedin.com/in/liviu-ghiuzan/

www.ingramcontent.com/pod-product-compliance
Lightning Source LLC
Chambersburg PA
CBHW051941290426
44110CB00015B/2070